Life in Nazi Germany

Hal Marcovitz

San Diego, CA

© 2015 ReferencePoint Press, Inc.
Printed in the United States

For more information, contact:
ReferencePoint Press, Inc.
PO Box 27779
San Diego, CA 92198
www.ReferencePointPress.com

LIBRARY OF CONGRESS CATALOGING-IN-PUBLICATION DATA

Marcovitz, Hal.
  Life in Nazi Germany / by Hal Marcovitz.
    pages cm. -- (Living history)
  Includes bibliographical references and index.
  ISBN-13: 978-1-60152-776-9 (hardback : alkaline paper)
  ISBN-10: 1-60152-776-4 (hardback : alkaline paper)
  1. National socialism--Juvenile literature. 2. Germany--History--1933-1945--Juvenile
literature. I. Title.
  DD256.5.M3335 2015
  943.086--dc23
                                                                        2014035264

Contents

Foreword

History is a complex and multifaceted discipline that embraces many different areas of human activity. Given the expansive possibilities for the study of history, it is significant that since the advent of formal writing in the Ancient Near East over six thousand years ago, the contents of most nonfiction historical literature have been overwhelmingly limited to politics, religion, warfare, and diplomacy.

Beginning in the 1960s, however, the focus of many historical works experienced a substantive change worldwide. This change resulted from the efforts and influence of an ever-increasing number of progressive contemporary historians who were entering the halls of academia. This new breed of academician, soon accompanied by many popular writers, argued for a major revision of the study of history, one in which the past would be presented from the ground up. What this meant was that the needs, wants, and thinking of ordinary people should and would become an integral part of the human record. As British historian Mary Fulbrook wrote in her 2005 book, *The People's State: East German Society from Hitler to Honecker,* students should be able to view "history with the people put back in." This approach to understanding the lives and times of people of the past has come to be known as social history. According to contemporary social historians, national and international affairs should be viewed not only from the perspective of those empowered to create policy but also through the eyes of those over whom power is exercised.

The American historian and best-selling author, Louis "Studs" Terkel, was one of the pioneers in the field of social history. He is best remembered for his oral histories, which were firsthand accounts of everyday life drawn from the recollections of interviewees who lived during pivotal events or periods in history. Terkel's first book, *Division Street America* (published in 1967), focuses on urban living in and around Chicago and is a compilation of seventy interviews of immigrants and native-born Americans. It was followed by several other oral histories including *Hard Times* (the 1930s depression), *Working* (people's feelings about their jobs), and his 1985 Pulitzer Prize–winning *The Good War* (about life in America before, during, and after World War II).

In keeping with contemporary efforts to present history by people and about people, ReferencePoint's *Living History* series offers students a journey through recorded history as recounted by those who lived it. While modern sources such as those found in *The Good War* and on radio and TV interviews are readily available, those dating to earlier periods in history are scarcer and often more obscure the further back in time one investigates. These important primary sources are there nonetheless waiting to be discovered in literary formats such as posters, letters, and diaries, and in artifacts such as vases, coins, and tombstones. And they are also found in places as varied as ancient Mesopotamia, Charles Dickens's England, and Nazi concentration camps. The *Living History* series uncovers these and other available sources as they relate the "living history" of real people to their student readers.

Important Events

1933
Adolf Hitler ascends to the chancellorship of Germany in a year in which the Gestapo is created, the Nazis burn books, and the first concentration camps are established.

1920
The Nazi Party of Germany adopts the swastika as its symbol.

1915	1920	1925	1930	1935

1918
World War I ends with the surrender of Germany.

1934
Hitler orders the murder of hundreds of political opponents in an episode known as the Night of the Long Knives.

1923
Nazi leader Adolf Hitler authors *Mein Kampf* (*My Struggle*) while serving a prison term for attempting to overthrow the German government.

1926
Nazi leaders create the Hitler Youth, an organization dedicated to indoctrinating young people into the principles of National Socialism.

1935
The propaganda film *Triumph des Willens* (*Triumph of the Will*) is produced, showing the strength of the German military and widespread public support for Nazism; also, the Nuremberg Laws are adopted, stripping Jews of their German citizenship.

6

in Nazi Germany

1936
The Gestapo is granted virtually unlimited authority to arrest and torture enemies of the *Reich*.

1940
The British Royal Air Force begins a bombing campaign of Berlin and other German cities.

1939
On September 1 German troops cross the border into Poland, touching off World War II.

1944
On June 6 the Allies launch a massive invasion of the European continent that leads to the retreat of the German army; in July advancing Soviet troops liberate the first Nazi concentration camp in Lublin, Poland.

| 1936 | 1938 | 1940 | 1942 | 1944 |

1938
On November 9 Nazi thugs vandalize Jewish homes and businesses in an episode known as *Kristallnacht* (Night of the Broken Glass).

1943
Due to the high number of young German men killed in battle, Nazi officials consider but ultimately reject a law encouraging adultery as a strategy for producing more babies.

1945
On April 30, as Allied and Soviet troops close in on Berlin, Hitler commits suicide; on May 8 the Allies declare VE (Victory in Europe) Day.

The Night the Nazis Burned the Books

On the night of May 10, 1933, some forty thousand people—many of them college students—gathered on the Opera Square in Berlin, a huge public square located next to the city's Humboldt University, for a bizarre ritual. Leaders of the Nazi Party had piled twenty-five thousand books in the square. As Nazi leaders made stirring speeches to the wild cheers of the crowd, the books were ignited, bursting into a conflagration that could be seen for blocks. That evening the scene was repeated on or near college campuses in thirty-three other German cities.

The night the Nazis burned the books marked a watershed moment in German history. It established what life would be like under the Nazi regime that had taken power just four months earlier when Adolf Hitler ascended to the chancellorship of Germany. The books represented the writings of authors considered "un-German"—those who encouraged readers to be freethinkers, to question authority, and to urge peaceful resolutions to international disputes. Among the writers whose books were burned that night were Socialists such as Bertolt Brecht and Karl Marx, whose views on investing power in the hands of the people ran counter to Hitler's belief in dictatorship. Books written by foreigners, such as Americans Ernest Hemingway and Jack London, were tossed into the blaze because the Nazis did not want Germans to read about the free will afforded to people in free societies. And finally, books written by Jews, including the internationally famous mathematician Albert Einstein and pioneering psychiatrist Sigmund Freud, were burned as well. The Nazis had targeted Jews for persecution and did not want the ideas of Jewish intellectuals polluting German thought.

As the books burned in Berlin, Joseph Goebbels, the German minister of propaganda, spoke to the crowd. He said, "The soul of the German people can again express itself. These flames not only illuminate the final end of an old era; they also light up the new."[1]

Nazi Thugs

Many of the university students who participated in the 1933 book burning formed lines around the bonfires. The students wore armbands displaying the initials SA, which stood for *Sturm Abteilung* (Storm Section)—a group of Nazi thugs who used strong-arm tactics to quell dissent. They passed books from the back of the lines to the front, where they were tossed into the blaze.

Erich Kästner stood in the crowd on the Opera Square, watching as books were thrown into the fire. Kästner was a poet and children's book author. A pacifist, he opposed the rise of National Socialism— the racist and warlike ideology championed by Hitler. (*Nazi* is the shortened German term for *National Socialist*.) In 1932 Kästner signed the Urgent Call for Unity, a statement calling on Germans to oppose Nazi candidates in that year's national election. The Urgent Call was signed by more than thirty well-known German authors, artists, and scientists. Among the books that were tossed into the blaze were those written by Kästner. Recalling the scene, he says,

> **WORDS IN CONTEXT**
> **Nazi**
> A follower of the political ideology championed by Adolf Hitler that was based on fierce nationalism, German supremacy, racial purity, and the goal of dominating the European continent.

> My books were burned with dark festive splendor in Berlin, on the large square next to the Opera, by a certain Mr. Goebbels. He triumphantly called out the names of twenty-four German writers, who symbolically had to be eradicated for eternity. I was the only one of the twenty-four who had appeared in person to witness this theatrical insolence.

I stood in front of the University, jammed between students in SA uniforms, the flower of the nation, saw our books lying in the flashing flames and listened to the sentimental tirades of the little consummate liar. Funeral weather hung over the town . . . It was disgusting.

Suddenly a shrill woman's voice called: "But that's Kästner standing there!" A young cabaret artist, pushing through the throng with a colleague, had seen me standing there and had given exaggerated expression to her astonishment. I became ill at ease. But nothing happened. (Although in those very days a great lot of things used to "happen.")[2]

Master Race

As Kästner and the other intellectuals of Germany had predicted, the Nazi regime quickly evolved into a despotic, totalitarian, and vindictive dictatorship. Those who did not share in Hitler's view of German supremacy were invariably arrested and tossed into concentration camps, where millions died. The Nazis dreamed of developing a "master race"—people of Northern European, or Aryan, ethnicity who represented exemplary physical specimens of humankind. To achieve this goal they aimed to cleanse German society of undesirables: Jews, but others as well—Slavs, Roma (then known as gypsies), Europeans of African descent, gays, political enemies, the mentally ill and physically disabled, and virtually anyone who defied their authority. The Nazis sought intellectual purity as well. Those who did not share in the Nazi vision were persecuted—among them Socialists and Communists, who believed that power should rest in the hands of the workers and not in the will of authoritarian overlords.

Moreover, during the Nazi era Hitler dreamed of making Germany the preeminent nation in Europe—and the world. Germany had

> **WORDS IN CONTEXT**
> **dictatorship**
> Form of government in which one person, the dictator, is provided with supreme authority.

Nazi Germany and Occupied Territories, 1944

emerged from World War I a demoralized nation. After it surrendered in 1918, its economy was in chaos. The government attempted to rebuild the nation and its industry but those efforts failed, leaving many Germans without jobs, homes, and food. These dire conditions provided fertile ground for the rise of Hitler and the Nazi Party. Hitler aimed to make European countries subservient to the *Reich*—the German realm. Soon after taking power in 1933 he began the process of rebuilding the German economy as well as the German military, which had been strictly limited in size under the terms of the Treaty of Versailles, which ended the war. Hitler looked toward spreading Nazi ideology hundreds of miles beyond Germany's borders. The Nazi dictator's campaign culminated in the 1939 invasion of neighboring Poland, which touched off World War II—a conflict that led to the deaths and displacement of tens of millions of people worldwide. The war ended in 1945 when the Allied armies defeated Germany, but not before the Nazis invaded and occupied a large swath of the European continent. In addition to portions of Poland, other countries that fell under Nazi occupation were Austria, Czechoslovakia, France, Holland, Belgium, Denmark, and Norway.

Following the mass book burning of 1933 the Nazis tightened their grip on German society, becoming more authoritarian while they prepared the German people, industry, and military for war. Most Germans readily accepted the loss of personal freedoms, the persecution of the Jews, and the militarization of their nation. Hitler was a dynamic and charismatic leader, and his plans for militarization created many jobs. And so, as the books burned that night, the German people found themselves blindly following the Nazis on a path toward destruction.

Chapter One

The Power of Propaganda

In 1923 Adolf Hitler found himself in a jail cell, sentenced to five years in prison for his role in organizing a failed coup against the government. (He did not have to serve the full sentence; he was paroled after nine months.) Hitler made good use of his time behind bars, dictating a book he titled *Mein Kampf* (*My Struggle*) to his cell mate and follower, Rudolf Hess.

In *Mein Kampf* Hitler laid out his plans for a future Germany and how he intended to seize control of the government. He devoted two chapters of the book to the use of propaganda, believing that to truly win over the allegiance of the German people he would have to provide them with a message they could embrace. Certainly, any civilized people could be expected to reject many of the notions expressed by Hitler in *Mein Kampf*—the racial purity of the German people; persecution of an entire ethnic group, the Jews; domination of the European continent; and the obliteration of all enemies. Nevertheless, Hitler believed that through the effective use of propaganda, he could persuade the German people to accept his ideas. In *Mein Kampf* he writes,

> The receptive powers of the masses are very restricted, and their understanding is feeble. On the other hand, they quickly forget. Such being the case, all effective propaganda must be confined to a few bare essentials and those must be expressed as far as possible in stereotyped formulas. These slogans should be persistently re-peated until the very last individual has come to grasp the idea that has been put forward.[3]

Ministry of Propaganda

Propaganda is misinformation masqueraded as the truth and disseminated to the public. Propaganda can be spread through paid advertisements, but throughout history propaganda has also been aired by news organizations that are aware of the mistruths but spread the lies because they are controlled by political or business leaders who believe in their mission.

After Hitler ascended to the chancellorship he rarely used the title "chancellor," the official position to which he had been appointed under the German constitution. Instead he preferred the title *Führer* (leader)— a title he had long used as head of the Nazi Party. In the German media Hitler was always referred to as Führer.

In fact, Hitler made control of the media a top priority. In March 1933 Hitler appointed Joseph Goebbels to the position of minister of propaganda. Regardless of the medium— newspapers, magazines, radio broadcasts, film—all content had to be approved by Goebbels's censors. To ensure that newspaper editors and others who disseminated information complied with Nazi standards, on October 3, 1933, the *Reichstäg*—the legislative branch of German government—passed the *Reich* Press Law. This law dictated that journalism would be regulated by the government. Moreover, all editors had to be German citizens and of Aryan descent. Jews were, of course, excluded. Even German editors married to Jews had to give up their jobs.

In Western democracies, such control of the press by government is unthinkable. As far back as the eighteenth century, the drafters of the US Constitution adopted the First Amendment, prohibiting government control over the press. America's Founding Fathers believed a free press is a vital component of a strong democracy.

But in Germany, Hitler wanted no such freedoms granted to the press. During the Nazi regime, editors of all German newspapers were summoned every morning to the local headquarters of the Ministry of Propaganda and told what news to report and how to report it: invariably, shining a favorable light on all Nazi activities.

Journalist William L. Shirer spent much of the 1930s in Berlin, covering the rise of the Nazi Party as a correspondent for American newspapers. Shirer reported that he was shocked by the German people's acceptance of the propaganda fed to them by the German government, believing all manners of lies as truth:

> No one who has not lived for years in a totalitarian land can possibly conceive how difficult it is to escape the dread consequences of the regime's calculated and incessant propaganda. Often in a German home or office or sometimes in a casual conversation with a stranger in a restaurant, a beer hall, a café, I would meet with the most outlandish assertions from seemingly educated and intelligent persons. It was obvious that they were parroting some piece of nonsense they had heard on the radio or read in the newspapers.[4]

The Attacker

The misleading and devious messages delivered by the Nazi propaganda machine were often targeted at Jews. From the earliest days of the Nazi regime, Jews were portrayed as money-driven capitalists intent on denying poor or working-class Germans their meager wages in favor of fattening their own wallets. Jews were portrayed as war profiteers—German businessmen who earned profits during World War I while millions of German soldiers died on the front lines.

Over the years much harsher images emerged, reflecting the Nazi perceptions of the Jews: immoral, indecent, dishonest, obese, ugly, subhuman—even cannibalistic. Much of the public's perception of Jews was orchestrated by the Nazi leader Julius Streicher, editor of the weekly tabloid newspaper *Der Stürmer* (*The Attacker*).

Der Stürmer was a particularly incendiary newspaper that portrayed Jews in the vilest terms; Jews, the newspaper insisted, were known to eat children and drink their blood. *Der Stürmer* was aimed at uneducated working-class Germans. Born in the German city of Cologne in 1928, Hebert Lutz recalls that as a boy he saw copies of *Der Stürmer* prominently

Der Stürmer, *the fiercely anti-Semitic tabloid newspaper, was a crucial part of the Nazi propaganda machine. Front-page headlines in a May 1934 edition read: "Jewish Murder Plan Against Non-Jewish Mankind Uncovered" and "The Jews Are Our Misfortune."*

displayed on newsstands and in magazine boxes across town. "It was real low-grade type of propaganda given to the people," Lutz says. "Truth didn't mean anything; distortion was enormous. It was almost like reading dirty fairy tales."[5]

German Jews felt wounded by their portrayal in *Der Stürmer* and similar publications. During the 1930s Stefanie Sucher lived in the German city of Nuremberg, where *Der Stürmer* was published. She lived near the newspaper's headquarters and walked by the building as she attended school in the home of a private tutor. (Starting in 1935 Jewish children were expelled from German public schools, forcing their parents to find private tutors for them.) "Very close to our building was the main building of *Der Stürmer*, the notorious Nazi newspaper," Sucher recalls.

I often had to pass this building on my way to some private lessons. . . . Once, while I glanced at their windows, I could see the front page of *Der Stürmer*, with a caricature of the Jews. I call it caricatures because they were. It was so bad and I saw them so often, that I later on felt that this must be what we are, that must be how we look, and it took me a long time to get rid of this image. . . . I had no feeling for myself. I actually ended up thinking that they were right, that I must look like . . . the caricatures in *Der Stürmer*. I thought that was my image, thought we were no good, that we didn't contribute to anything, that we were inferior.[6]

Hardened Hearts

Conditions for Jews in Germany grew much worse. By the end of the decade they had lost their rights of citizenship, and their property had been confiscated by the German government. Jews who had not fled to other countries were rounded up and sent to concentration camps where they were made to do slave labor, given little food, and often succumbed to starvation or disease or were forced to die in Nazi gas chambers. Ordinary German citizens played a role in these crimes against the Jewish people: Germans who served in the army or police agencies, Germans who worked as camp guards, and Germans who alerted Nazi authorities to Jews in hiding, among others. The image of the Jews that had been created for years by the incessant Nazi propaganda hardened their hearts, making it easy for them to turn on their Jewish neighbors.

Says Kurt Möbius, a German police officer who served at a concentration camp in Chelmno, Poland: "I was then of the conviction that the Jews were not innocent but guilty. I believed the propaganda that all Jews were criminals and subhumans and that they were the cause of Germany's decline after the First World War. The thought that one should disobey or evade the order to participate in the extermination of the Jews did not therefore enter my mind at all."[7]

The Nazis even included an anti-Jewish lyric in their party's anthem, "Horst Wessel–Lied" ("Horst Wessel's Song"). The anthem was written in 1929 by Horst Wessel, commander of an SA division in Berlin. A year after writing the song Wessel was murdered in a crime that was never solved (although the Nazis blamed a local Communist cell). Nazi officials made Wessel into a martyr and adopted the song he wrote as their party's anthem. After Hitler seized power in 1933 "Horst Wessel–Lied" was considered a co-national anthem of Germany, along with the familiar "Deutschlandlied," or "Song of Germany." During parades and other public events, Nazis sang "Horst Wessel–Lied" with tremendous gusto. The song includes these lyrics:

> When Jewish blood flows from the knife
> Then everything goes so well.[8]

Ideal Aryans

Hitler's propaganda machine did not just plant disturbing images of Jews in the public mind. It also worked very hard to paint a portrait of the ideal Aryan man and woman. Throughout Berlin and other cities, public walls were plastered with Nazi Party posters portraying images of Aryan men and women—invariably young, wholesome, athletic, and healthy. Women were often portrayed as blondes, their hair usually

A 1934 German public information brochure promotes the ideal Aryan family, with the headline: "Healthy Parents—Healthy Children!" Walls throughout German cities were plastered with Nazi Party posters like this one.

tied into pigtails. Such images were often accompanied by optimistic Nazi slogans, extolling the virtues of hard work, sacrifice, and dedication to Germany and the Nazi vision. Among the common slogans found on Nazi posters were:

The *Reich* will never be destroyed if you are united and loyal.

Long live Germany!

No one shall go hungry! No one shall be cold!

Don't give. Sacrifice.

Before: Unemployment, hopelessness, desolation, strikes, lockouts. Today: Work, joy, discipline, camaraderie.

We build body and soul.[9]

Many of the posters featured heroic images of Hitler. Artists doctored the portrait of the Führer, giving Hitler broader shoulders, a trimmer waist, and, generally, a more athletic physique than what the middle-aged dictator (he was forty-three years old when he took power in early 1933) had in real life. Hitler was usually portrayed with a stern and earnest expression, sending a message to the German people that he took his responsibilities seriously. Among the slogans readers could find under his portrait were:

Let Hitler work!

Hitler Builds

Be true to the Führer.

Führer, we will follow you.

One People, One *Reich*, One Führer.[10]

Some of the posters featuring portraits of the Führer included quotations from his speeches. "I ask the German people to strengthen my faith and to lend me its strength so that I will always and everywhere have the strength to fight for its honor and freedom, to work for its economic prosperity, and particularly to strengthen me in my struggles for genuine peace,"[11] read one popular poster plastered throughout German cities.

In Their Own Words

Witnessing the Nazi Salute

Martha Dodd, daughter of William Dodd, the American ambassador to Nazi Germany, describes the Hitler salute as she witnessed it in 1939. The salute was performed at a diplomatic function at the American embassy by German foreign minister Joachim von Ribbentrop. (At the time, the United States was not yet at war with Nazi Germany.) Says Dodd,

The first time I met von Ribbentrop was at a luncheon we gave at the Embassy. He was tall and slender, with a vague handsomeness. Outstanding among all the guests, Ribbentrop arrived in Nazi uniform. Most Nazis came to diplomatic functions in ordinary suits unless the affair was extremely formal. His manner of shaking hands was an elaborate ceremony in itself. He held out his hand, then retreated and held your hand at arm's length, lowered his arm stiffly by his side, then raised the arm swiftly in a Nazi salute, just barely missing your nose. All the time he was staring at you with such intensity you were wondering what new sort of mesmerism he thought he was effecting. The whole ritual was performed with such self-conscious dignity and such silence that hardly a word was whispered while Ribbentrop made his exhibitionist acquaintance with the guests present. To me the procedure was so ridiculous I could scarcely keep a straight face.

Quoted in Tilman Allert, *The Hitler Salute: On the Meaning of a Gesture.* New York: Picador, 2005, pp. 48–49.

Erwin Hammel, a Cologne teenager during the 1930s, says German citizens accepted the propaganda of the posters—and the propaganda published by the news media as well—because the Nazis were able to close off news from foreign outlets. Newspapers and magazines published outside Germany were forbidden, and few Germans owned radios powerful enough to pick up foreign, uncensored broadcasts. Hammel explains:

> As children, we didn't have the opportunity to travel, so we didn't get to know Germany from another point of view. We didn't have that at all. This made the propaganda that we were exposed to seem very plausible. We heard and saw nothing else. . . . We didn't have the opportunity to hear about the world abroad. There were no foreign newspapers, and so on. Today you can go to any kiosk and buy an American or English newspaper, or a Polish one or whatever, and you can read what others think about us. But back then we didn't have any such opportunity.[12]

Nazi Symbols

The posters that displayed young Aryan men and women often depicted them giving the Nazi salute—also known as the Hitler salute. The salute was performed by raising the right arm, outstretched and rigid. It was originally adopted by Nazi Party members in 1923 to salute Hitler, who by then had taken over a fringe political organization composed of beer hall thugs and disillusioned and unemployed World War I veterans. After the Nazis took power in 1933 Germans routinely used the salute as a greeting. The salute was incorporated into propaganda posters but also all manner of other public art: Historians have unearthed a painting, found in a Nazi-era school, depicting a scene from the fairy tale *Snow White*. The painting depicts the prince greeting Snow White with the Nazi salute.

The salute was more than just a silent gesture of respect toward the German nation as well as its leader. The salute was often performed as the citizen uttered the phrase *"Sieg Heil!"* ("Hail Victory!"). The phrase

"*Heil Hitler!*" ("Hail Hitler!") was also spoken, sharply and distinctly, to honor the Nazi leader.

In 1935 a young member of a German rowing club in the city of Konstanz was scolded by friends when he delivered the salute without speaking the words "*Heil Hitler!*" He says, "One evening in early 1935, when I showed up at the clubhouse for practice and greeted others—as I always had—with the familiar *Salut*, an aggressive young kid said, 'Don't you know that the proper German greeting is '*Heil Hitler!*' I thought he was joking and looked around at my teammates, but there was only awkward silence. No one batted an eyelash. There was no mistake. The kid was serious. Without a word, I went to my locker and packed my things. I left the club and never returned."[13]

The Nazi salute as well as the swastika—the emblem of the Nazi Party—were symbols, and Hitler well understood the power of symbols for propaganda purposes. (The swastika, or hooked cross, had been a familiar symbol—used as far back as ancient Greece. Over the centuries various civilizations regarded the hooked cross as a symbol for peace.) Hitler appreciated the striking look of the emblem and in 1920 ordered it adopted as the symbol of the Nazi Party. After Hitler and the Nazis took power in 1933, red flags bearing the swastika were unfurled throughout Germany.

> **WORDS IN CONTEXT**
> **swastika**
> A hooked cross traditionally used as a symbol for peacc; adapted as the symbol of the Nazi Party, the swastika represented Nazi culture and Hitler's intentions to rule over the European continent.

Nazi Films

These symbols of Nazi Germany—the salute as well as the swastika—were perhaps most prominently displayed in the films produced by Nazi-era moviemakers. In America, Great Britain, and the other Western democracies, filmmaking exploded in the 1930s as sound was adapted to movies and cinemas attracted long lines of fans. Film-going was also a hugely popular pastime in Germany, and the Nazis realized that an effective way to spread their message was through the medium of film.

At a 1933 rally, members of the Hitler Youth raise their right arms in the traditional Nazi salute. The salute was one of many symbols that helped galvanize public support for the Nazis.

As with all forms of expression, filmmaking was watched closely by Goebbels and the Ministry of Propaganda, which held the power of approval over all scripts. Controlling the content of films enabled the Nazis to prepare the German people for one of the regime's main goals—rebuilding and rearming the German military. Indeed, soon after taking over the government Hitler laid plans to enlarge the German army, which under the terms of the Treaty of Versailles was limited to no more than one hundred thousand troops. And so the Nazis began a program to rebuild the Germany army into a formidable fighting force and to arm the troops with modern weapons. The program to rebuild and rearm the German army was known as *Aufrüstung* (armament).

At the Propaganda Ministry Goebbels put his unique talents to work selling ordinary Germans—particularly young German men—on the importance of a powerful German army. The most blatant example of pro-*Aufrüstung* propaganda could be found in the 1935 film *Triumph des Willens* (*Triumph of the Will*) directed by Hitler's favorite filmmaker, Leni Riefenstahl. The theatrical poster for the film left little doubt of the contents: It features a German soldier holding a Nazi flag, and the soldier wears an expression of serious resolve. Hitler was so delighted with the film that he ordered his name placed in the opening credits as executive producer.

The film depicts bucolic scenes of Germany while classical music— written by German composers—plays in the background. An airplane arrives at the city of Nuremberg. Hitler and other Nazi leaders emerge from the plane to the thunderous applause of thousands of people. The film depicts military parades and a rally held by young people. Making a speech during the rally, Hitler declares that military service is a noble calling and that they must harden themselves and prepare for sacrifice. The film concludes as Hitler addresses a rally attended by some 150,000 soldiers. At the conclusion of the speech, the soldiers raise their arms in the Nazi salute and shout, in unison, "*Sieg Heil! Sieg Heil!*"

Prior to the filming Hitler gave specific orders to Riefenstahl: "I don't want a boring Party rally film; I don't want newsreel shots. I want an artistic visual document."[14] Although the film was unquestionably a propaganda device, Riefenstahl proved herself a talented filmmaker able to portray Hitler at his most charismatic. Moreover, it showed the German army as a powerful, united, and dedicated force—and that it was the moral responsibility of every young German man to serve his country in the military. A German movie critic, writing in the magazine *Die Film-woche* (*The Film Week*) comments on the film: "What matters in this film

Looking Back

The Value of Symbols

Years before taking control of the German government, Adolf Hitler realized the value of propaganda and, in particular, the use of symbols to capture the attention of the German people. Klaus P. Fischer, professor of history at Hancock College in California, explains that Hitler—who as a young man aspired to enter art school—even took a hand in designing the Nazi flags. Says Fischer:

> Hitler . . . possessed a keen psychological and aesthetic appreciation of the unifying power of symbols in political life. He would spend hours on end thumbing through art magazines and the heraldic departments of the Munich State Library to find the right eagle for the standard rubber stamp of the [Nazi] party. About the same time that the swastika became the official symbol of the party, Josef Fuess, a jeweler, was commissioned by Hitler to design the party's official badge. Party armbands, displaying the swastika in the same manner depicted on the flags, came into being shortly afterward, and Hitler insisted that all party members wear such insignia during duty hours. By the end of 1922, Hitler also designed the . . . banners for the SA. These [banners] were adorned with an eagle perched atop an encircled swastika; below that was a rectangular party shield (or local party shield) to which was affixed the party banner with swastika and the slogan, "Germany Awaken."

Klaus P. Fischer, *Nazi Germany: A New History.* New York: Continuum, 1995, p. 130.

is not the chronological progression of the [Nuremberg] rally—what matters is something more important: making visible and tangible the electrifying rhythm of the greatest movement of the people that has ever taken place on German soil."[15] A glowing review, to be sure, but one that nevertheless had to meet the approval of Goebbels's censors before it could be published.

The Ultimate Sacrifice

Triumph of the Will helped the Nazis achieve their goal. By the summer of 1939, as Hitler prepared to invade neighboring Poland, the German military consisted of some 4.2 million combatants. These men had come of age during an era when the Nazi government controlled the content of the newspapers and magazines they read, the posters they saw plastered across their cities, and the dialogue they heard spoken by their favorite actors and actresses. By the outbreak of the war most German citizens accepted the Nazi vision that the Aryan race was destined to dominate the European continent. Now, as soldiers of the German army, they were expected to make the ultimate sacrifice—to die in battle, if necessary—to ensure that Hitler's vision for the future became a reality.

Chapter Two

The Police State

In 1933 Adolf Hitler's top deputy, Hermann Goering, created a secret police force designed to terrorize political opponents of the Nazi Party. Goering intended to use strong-arm tactics to stifle dissent. He proposed to call the police force the *Geheimes Polizei Amt* (Secret Police Office) but was troubled by the initials for the organization: GPA. It sounded too much like GPU, which stood for *Gosudarstvennoye Politicheskoye Upravlenie*—the Soviet secret police. (The Nazis despised the Soviet Union, which they considered a nation of inferiors: Slavs and Communists.)

An obscure post office employee in Berlin solved Goering's naming problem. Goering sent aides to the post office to create a franking stamp—a stamp that would provide his new organization with free postage. The postal worker, whose name has been lost to history, suggested the organization's name be changed to *Geheime Staatspolizei* (Secret State Police). Moreover, the name could easily be abbreviated to fit on the franking stamp. The abbreviation: Gestapo.

Rooting Out Enemies

And so, in these most humble of circumstances, a name was created for an organization that reflected the most hideous aspects of the Nazi regime: an evil and sadistic organization of thugs and killers who, with no qualms or pangs of conscience, readily resorted to torture, imprisonment, and murder in its mission to stamp out dissent and ensure the enemies of the *Reich* were silenced. To accomplish these goals the Nazi regime sought its most dedicated, and hard-hearted, devotees as recruits for the Gestapo. Although all police departments in Germany were placed under the authority of the Gestapo starting in 1936, only the most ardent

Nazis were given special status as Gestapo agents and tasked with rooting out enemies of the regime. "Unquestioning devotion to the Nazi cause to the point of complete oblivion to human rights is a prerequisite," wrote *New York Times* correspondent Philip Whitman in 1942. "The men who carry out Gestapo orders must be hard and unwavering in their obedience. They are more than policemen, for they do not deal with ordinary crime and the punishment thereof. They are political police, with a task far more delicate than that of fighting crime, for the suspects they must watch, arrest and see condemned are often upright citizens by any criminal code."[16]

Reinhard Heydrich fit that mold. Born in 1904, Heydrich grew up in an affluent household, listening to his parents rail against Jews. Being raised in such an environment, he became a virulent anti-Semite himself. During his brief career as a German naval officer Heydrich became a dedicated Nazi and in 1934 was recruited to join the Gestapo. His ardent belief in the Nazi mission, his disdain for Jews, and his cold methods of carrying out his duties all helped him rise swiftly in the ranks. In 1939 he was made a deputy commander of the Gestapo. In 1940 Gestapo agent Hansjürgen Koehler described his boss:

> **WORDS IN CONTEXT**
> *polizei*
> The German word for *police*.

> Heydrich is young and intelligent. . . . In short, he is the brutal, despotic and merciless master of the Nazi police; a go-getter, whose hard certainty of aim knows no deviation. . . . Although he is hot-blooded and impetuous himself, he remains soberly, coldly calculating in the background and knows that the power he coveted is already his. Cruelty and sudden rage are just as severely disciplined in his make-up as his untiring activity.[17]

The arrest and murder of Margarete Leib's father illustrates the tactics devised by Heydrich and other leaders of the Gestapo. In March 1933 Leib's father was a member of the *Reichstäg*, the German lawmaking body. He was a member of the Social Democratic Party, which lost its elected majority in the *Reichstäg* two months earlier to the Nazis. Now that the Nazis were in power, they intended to silence critics—particularly politicians who opposed the Nazi movement. Leib says her father was arrested by the Gestapo in his Berlin home and imprisoned in a concentration camp.

He was held in the camp for a year. Leib and her mother were allowed to visit him occasionally and bring him meals. In March 1934, though, Leib learned her father was dead. "They strangled him with a packaging cord," she said later. "But so they could conceal what had happened, they hung him from a window frame and then called a doctor."[18] A few days later Berlin newspapers reported that Leib's father had committed suicide—a story concocted by the Gestapo, Leib believes.

Night of the Long Knives

By the time of Leib's father's murder, such tactics by police in Nazi Germany were common. In fact, they had been used by the Nazis even before they seized power. In 1921 the Nazis, then a rising political force in Germany, created the SA to serve as the party's security wing. Known as "Stormtroopers" or "Brownshirts" because of the color of their uniforms, SA members were mostly beer hall roughnecks who roamed the streets looking for fights. They could always be counted on to silence opponents of Nazism—safe in the assurance that as they broke windows, burned shops, and smashed bones, the police looked the other way.

But in 1934, after he assumed power, Hitler feared that the head of the SA, Ernst Röhm, was growing too powerful. On June 30 the Führer had Röhm and hundreds of others he suspected of duplicity murdered. The arrests and murders of Röhm and the others is known as *Nacht der Langen Messer* ("Night of the Long Knives"; the term is a German expression for an act of vengeance and has its roots in a fifth-century German mythological tale about the massacre of a king's army). The incident marked a turning point in German history, for Hitler seized on the moment to declare himself the absolute judge of guilt and innocence in German society—a right he reserved for himself in a speech to the *Reichstäg* the following night. And to carry out his vindictiveness toward the people he perceived as enemies of the *Reich*, Hitler invested wide-ranging powers in the national police forces he created.

After the murder of Röhm, Hitler replaced him with a close aide, Heinrich Himmler. Under Himmler the SA was merged into the *Schutzstaffel* (Protection Squadron) or SS. Hitler created the SS in 1925, designating the unit as his personal bodyguard. It grew into a formidable force of thugs and roughnecks vehemently loyal to the Nazi leader. Even in the SS, however, an organization composed of the most devout and coldhearted Nazis,

Members of the Nazi Party's security wing, the **Sturm Abteilung** *(also known as SA or Brownshirts) march in a 1933 parade. SA members were mostly thugs who broke windows, burned shops, and smashed bones.*

some officers stood out as especially vindictive and devious. In 1933 these men were recruited for a new division within the SS: the Gestapo.

The Gestapo and the Jews

Margarete Leib's father was a member of the *Reichstäg*, and therefore he held a politically powerful post—clearly, the type of figure whom the Nazis wanted to silence. But eventually all enemies of the Nazi regime—particularly Jews—found themselves hunted down by the Gestapo. Erich Hopp had worked as a journalist in Berlin until Germany stripped the country's Jews of their rights and forced them out of the professions. Like thousands of others, Hopp lost his job, but by 1942 he had found work as a laborer. By then Jews were the victims of intense persecution—those who had not found a way to leave Germany on their own were being deported to Poland and other countries, where they faced imprisonment and likely death in concentration camps. Hopp recalls the night the Gestapo came for him; his wife, Charlotte; and fourteen-year-old son, Wolfgang:

> About nine o'clock the doorbell rang—an unusual hour for visitors. I started to answer it, but Wolfgang stopped me. "Don't open it, don't," he whispered. The bell rang again then we heard a letter drop in the mailbox.
>
> We found a large envelope which contained the dreaded message: prepare to be evacuated. We were to be allowed to take a few things with us, including toilet articles, a blanket, and one change of clothes.
>
> All night we weighed our chances for life. If we avoided deportation, how could we get along without a place to live . . . always in danger of being reported by self-appointed denouncers? But deportation meant at best a precarious living and perhaps death.[19]

Hopp and his family decided to fake their own suicides and go underground. They left a suicide note in their apartment and escaped that night. Later, Hopp learned the Gestapo arrived at the apartment at six o'clock the next morning, and when no one answered the door the agents

As part of an early campaign to eliminate Jewish businesses, members of the SA block the entrance to a Jewish-owned shop in Berlin in 1933. The sign in the middle reads: "Germans! Defend Yourselves! Don't Buy from Jews!"

broke in. They found the suicide note and believed the story. Hopp says he also learned that if his family had been arrested, they would have been part of a roundup and deportation orchestrated by the Gestapo of some three thousand Jews. Upon arrival in Poland all Jews—men, women, and children—were executed. "We would have been dead if we had not gone underground,"[20] says Hopp.

Prinz Albrecht Strasse 8

Hopp and his family were able to escape the Gestapo; for those who were arrested, their first stop was typically the basement of Gestapo headquarters, a former Berlin art school located at the address of Prinz Albrecht Strasse 8. In the years in which the Nazis held power, thousands of victims were rounded up and tossed into cells in the building's basement, where they were tortured and often murdered.

Prinz Albrecht Strasse was a most unlikely street to find a center for torture. Located in one of Berlin's most fashionable neighborhoods, the "Alex" or the "Hotel Prinz Albrecht"—as it was derisively known by those who were arrested by the Gestapo—was surrounded by museums and ornate office buildings. The five-story sandstone building featured an elegant stone staircase and courtyard. When the Gestapo took over, the police agency rebuilt the interior, adding a warren of cells to the basement.

Gestapo arrests were typically executed at dawn. The unfortunate suspect was greeted with a pounding at his or her door accompanied by the shout of "*Gestapo! Aufmachen!*" ("Gestapo! Open up!") Upon answering the door, the suspect found Gestapo agents, invariably dressed in black leather trench coats and wide-brimmed fedora hats pulled down low over their eyes. To identify themselves the Gestapo agents flashed oval metal badges, one side bearing the image of the Nazi eagle, the other side the words *Geheime Staatspolizei*. Under German law the Gestapo agents were not required to provide suspects with their names or further identification.

> **WORDS IN CONTEXT**
> *Aufmachen!*
> Open up!

After being handcuffed the suspect was then shoved into a waiting automobile and driven to Gestapo headquarters on Prinz Albrecht Strasse. If family members were home during the moment of arrest, the Gestapo agents did not tell them of their loved one's destination. But virtually everyone who had witnessed a Gestapo arrest in Berlin knew the arrestees were imprisoned at Prinz Albrecht Strasse 8. They also knew that visiting arrestees at Gestapo headquarters was not allowed. Says Whitman, the *New York Times* correspondent, "When a Berliner says, 'He has gone to the Prinz Albrecht Strasse' he is likely to shrug his shoulders in a gesture signifying hopelessness."[21]

The Techniques of Torture

The mission of the Gestapo, as well as the SS, was to ensure that dissent against the Nazi regime was silenced. Upon arrival at Prinz Albrecht Strasse 8, long lists of charges, including treason, were often lodged against arrestees,

In Their Own Words

Medieval Torture

In 1944 a group of army officers attempted to assassinate Adolf Hitler. The Nazi regime foiled the plot, arresting, executing, and imprisoning dozens of conspirators. One conspirator, Fabian von Schlabrendorff, describes his torture:

> A device which gripped all the fingers separately was fastened to my hands. The inner side of this mechanism was studded with pins whose points pressed against my fingertips. The turning of a screw caused the instrument to contract, thus forcing the pin points into my fingers.
>
> When that did not achieve the desired confession . . . I was strapped, face down, on a frame resembling a bedstead, and my head was covered with a blanket. Then cylinders resembling stovepipes studded with nails on their inner surface were shoved over my bare legs. Here, too, a screw mechanism was used to contract the tubes so that the nails pierced my legs from ankle to thigh.
>
> For the third stage of torture, the "bedstead" itself was the main instrument. I was strapped down as described above, again with a blanket over my head. With the help of a special mechanism this medieval torture rack was then expanded . . . stretching my shackled body.
>
> In the fourth and final stage I was tied in a bent position which did not allow me to move even slightly backwards or sideways. Then [Gestapo agents] together fell on me from behind and beat me with heavy clubs. Each blow caused me to fall forward, and because my hands were chained behind my back, I crashed with full force on my face.

Quoted in Roger Moorhouse, *Berlin at War*. New York: Basic Books, 2010, pp. 235–36.

who were expected to confess. Believing themselves innocent, most suspects were hesitant to do so. Moreover, Gestapo agents demanded identities of co-conspirators. Certainly, people who believed themselves innocent did not want to bring down the force of the Gestapo on their friends.

But the Gestapo had ways of making people talk. Among the techniques used in the basement of Prinz Albrecht Strasse 8 were whippings with a lash; immersion, headfirst, in a tub of icy water; electrical shocks administered to the head, feet, fingers, and genitals; crushing genitals in a hand-cranked vise; and burning body parts with open flames, usually administered with

Nazi authorities arrest factory leaders around 1943. The Gestapo rarely told family members where their loved ones were being taken, but in Berlin most people knew they would end up in the torture chambers of Gestapo headquarters at Prinz Albrecht Strasse 8.

matches or soldering torches. Also, a suspect's hands might be handcuffed behind his or her back, then hoisted high with a rope strung through a pulley—causing intense pressure and pain on the spine and shoulders.

Anybody suspected of opposing the Nazi regime feared arrest and torture at Prinz Albrecht Strasse 8. The Gestapo could even come knocking with the intent to arrest a teenage girl. That is the fate that nearly awaited Anne Marie Reuss, a resident of the Berlin suburb of Steglitz. Evidence had reached Prinz Albrecht Strasse 8 that Anne Marie was among a group of teenagers overheard singing a satirical song about the Hitler Youth, the national youth group that all young Germans were expected to join. The lyrics of the official Hitler Youth song read, "Our flag flutters before us. . . . Into the future we go, man for man." But Anne Marie and her friends were overhead singing a version of the lyrics satirizing the plump Baldur von Schirach, the national leader of the Hitler Youth: "Our Baldur wobbles before us. . . . Our Baldur is a fatty."[22]

The Gestapo did not regard the antics of Anne Marie and her friends as harmless fun. Under German law satirizing the Hitler Youth was considered a crime, and so one morning Anne Marie's astonished mother answered the door to find Gestapo agents intending to arrest her daughter. When Anne Marie's mother was told the reason, she protested that her family was loyal to the Nazis, pointing to a portrait of Hitler hanging in the Reuss home. "Look gentlemen," she said, "we have a picture of the Führer hanging here."[23] Luckily for Anne Marie, she was not home at the time. The Gestapo men left, but not before declaring that Anne Marie should be informed of their visit. They did not return.

Nazi Prisons

Had Anne Marie and her friends been taken into custody, it is likely the teenagers would have been incarcerated in a Nazi prison. Typically, inmates held in Nazi prisons were crammed into unsanitary cells, provided with little food, and often tortured. A typical prison of the era could be found in the town of Sonnenburg in a region of central Germany known as Hesse.

In 1934 an anonymous author who claimed to have escaped from Sonnenburg wrote an essay about his experiences for the *Farmers Weekly*, a

Looking Back

National Comrades and Community Aliens

In creating a police state in Nazi Germany, Adolf Hitler divided Germans into two groups: those who were loyal to the regime (national comrades) and enemies who had to be rooted out (community aliens). Explains University of London history professor Nikolaus Wachsmann,

> From the beginning, terror was a principal feature of the . . . Reich. Of course, not the entire population was targeted directly. Nazi society was divided into friend and foe. On the one hand, "national comrades" were supposed to be protected by the state and encouraged to procreate, with the ultimate aim of creating a socially, politically and racially regimented community, an image incessantly perpetrated by Nazi propaganda. "Community aliens," on the other hand, had to be singled out and removed from Nazi society. Hitler made clear that all those who did not, or could not, fit in had to be brutally attacked. In a speech before the Reichstag on 23 March 1933, in the debate that marked the official end of parliamentarism in Germany, Hitler demanded that "in future, treason against the country and the *Volk* [people] should be burned out with barbaric ruthlessness." His announcement was greeted with ecstatic applause by [*Reichstäg* members]. Of course, such threats also served as a warning to "national comrades" not to step out of line. Deterrence was always a central element of Nazi policy.

Nikolaus Wachsmann, *Hitler's Prisons: Legal Terror in Nazi Germany*. New Haven, CT: Yale University Press, 2004, p. 68.

Communist newspaper. In his essay, the escaped prisoner described Sonnenburg as a penitentiary once reserved for Germany's most notorious criminals but later used by the Nazis to house political prisoners—among them Communists, Jews, and opponents of the regime. He writes: "In the month of April 1933 the first group of prisoners, I among them, was transported to the camp of Sonnenburg under the vigilance of police and Nazi shock troops. For hours and hours we remained standing in open (railroad) cars. . . . Our arrival at the [prison] was greeted first by the warden, a Nazi of the most savage variety, and pistols—triggers cocked—were pointed at us. Immediately we heard: 'You communist pigs! Keep your filthy heads up. Hey there, stand at attention you blockhead.' Then comes the order to sing the National Anthem."[24]

Led into the camp, the escaped prisoner reported that the inmates felt the brutality of the guards immediately: "The [guards] beat the prisoners with the butts of their guns and strike them across the face with fists. Those who do not march in step are kicked in the shins with heavy hob-nailed boots. . . . Everywhere we meet gloomy faces, seldom do we see a smile. So, assailed on every side by oaths, kicks, and blows, we arrive at the prison courtyard. Our pockets are searched. We are told to write home that we are very well treated; if we don't we are warned the consequences will be our heads."[25]

Digging Their Own Graves

The typical day at Sonnenburg began at five o'clock in the morning when the prisoners were roused out of their cells and forced to do calisthenics and military-style marching drills. The escaped inmate describes some of the individual treatments endured by fellow inmates:

Former communist members of [the *Reichstäg,* including] the lawyer Litten, were beaten for hours in their cells until their bodies were covered with blood. Schindler was forced to count every blow he received. Obuch was so badly wounded, that he is now unable to walk but it was Willi Kasper who received by far the worst treatment since the Nazis seem determined to torture him to death.

A Jewish shopkeeper, Rudi Bernstein, had to be sent to the state hospital in Berlin as a result of the blows he received. Karl von Ossietzky, the author and editor, though already in a very bad physical condition when he arrived at Sonnenburg, was as badly treated as the others. The writer, Erich Muehsam, had all the hairs of his head and beard plucked out. When he was brought back to us none of us recognized him.

In April, Willi Kasper [and] Erich Muehsam were sent to dig their own graves near the wall of the prison court. The other prisoners were taken out into the yard to watch their comrades being beaten and generally mistreated. Only the last-minute intervention of an officer who arrived from Berlin . . . saved the prisoners from the firing squad.[26]

Unchallenged Authority

The evil and sadistic tactics of the SS and Gestapo were entirely legal under German law. On February 10, 1936, the *Reichstäg* passed a law stating, "Neither the instructions nor the affairs of the Gestapo will be open to review by the administrative courts."[27] Moreover, Hitler himself provided the Gestapo with virtually unlimited powers in dealing with subversives and all others considered enemies of the *Reich*. In 1938 he declared, "All means, even if they are not in conformity with existing laws and precedents, are legal if they subserve the will of the Führer."[28]

Hitler believed he had to establish a police state in Germany to fulfill his ultimate goal of controlling his country's people. To prepare his country for war against Germany's neighbors, Hitler tolerated no internal dissent. During the Nazi era millions of Germans endured imprisonment, torture, and death at the hands of the agents of the Gestapo and SS, enabling Hitler to pursue his plans for European domination secure in the knowledge that he faced no challenge to his authority at home.

Chapter Three

Jewish Life in German Cities

From 1909 to 1913 Adolf Hitler lived as a pauper in the Austrian city of Vienna. He worked in a variety of menial jobs—shoveling snow, carrying baggage at a train station, and beating the dirt out of carpets. He slept in flophouses and took his meals at charity soup kitchens. During this period of his life Hitler befriended a man named Neumann. Although Neumann had a skill—polishing copper pots—and thus a little income, he took his meals at the same soup kitchens as Hitler. But Neumann frequently had a few coins in his pocket and never hesitated to lend them to his friend. On one bitterly cold Vienna day Neumann gave Hitler his overcoat.

Neumann, perhaps the only friend Hitler made during his years in Vienna, was a Jew. Hitler's friendship with Neumann is considered one of history's most puzzling ironies: During this most dismal period of his life, only a Jew reached out to Hitler in friendship—and yet the future chancellor of Germany evolved into a rabid anti-Semite who eventually ordered a campaign of genocide that extinguished the lives of some 6 million Jews. "Wherever I went [in Vienna]," he wrote later, "I began to see Jews, and the more I saw, the more sharply they became distinguished in my eyes from the rest of humanity. . . . Later, I often grew sick to the stomach from the smell of these caftan-wearers."[29]

> **WORDS IN CONTEXT**
> **genocide**
> Deliberate killing of a people who belong to a particular national, ethnic, racial, or religious group.

Jews Ignore the Warnings

By the time Hitler took power in 1933 the German people knew his feelings about Jews. During the growth of the Nazi Party in the 1920s and early 1930s, Hitler railed against the Jews—blaming them for the poverty that afflicted the German people and insisting that wealthy Jewish industrialists profited from Germany's militarism during World War I. Hitler realized that to build support for the Nazi Party he needed to identify an enemy—villains to blame for the nation's ills. Hitler believed he could stir passions against Jews.

Incredibly, many Jews failed to comprehend the implications of Hitler's rise to power. Many Jews were, themselves, veterans of the German army and felt betrayed by the German government and Treaty of Versailles. They, too, wished for Germany to return to a position of strength on the European continent.

Moreover, during the 1920s many wealthy Jews worried about the rise of the German Communist movement. They feared that if Communists took control of the government, the banks and factories, many under the ownership of Jews, would be nationalized—meaning the government would take them over. "Some of those German Jews were more German than Jews," says William Benson, a German Jew from the city of Leipzig whose family fled Germany in 1937. "They had medals and they were real gung-ho—real, real Germans, especially the rich ones—because Hitler was against communism. Anybody with money would say, 'Oh, good, Hitler. He's a good guy to have around.'"[30]

> **WORDS IN CONTEXT**
>
> **truncheon**
>
> A short baton or club typically carried by police officers.

First Camps

The attitudes of most Jews started changing soon after Hitler took power in early 1933. Violence and inhumanity against Jews occurred openly on the streets of German cities. Max Abraham, a Berlin rabbi, relates this story:

> When I heard from a friend for the first time in March of 1933 what he had seen from the window of his apartment in Berlin

. . . how Nazis beat Jews terribly with rubber truncheons and cut off their beards . . . I just could not believe it—even though I was convinced that my friend would never lie. He went on to tell me that Nazi thugs had forced their way into a nearby synagogue, forced those who were praying to lie down on the benches, and mistreated them. . . . Other friends living nearby confirmed his account. Soon I experienced, physically, firsthand the terrible barbarism that had befallen Germany.[31]

That barbarism was revealed in April 1933 when the Nazis erected the first concentration camps near the German cities of Dachau, Buchenwald, Sachsenhausen, Papenburg, and Ravensbrück. Built to house political enemies of the *Reich*, soon they were populated primarily

German soldiers jeer as a Jewish boy is forced to cut his father's beard in 1933. Insults, aggression, and outright violence occurred openly against German Jews once Hitler came to power.

with Jews. Eventually millions of Jews (and other "undesirables") were processed through a network of some twenty thousand labor camps, concentration camps, and killing centers located in Germany, Poland, Czechoslovakia, Ukraine, and other Nazi-occupied countries in eastern Europe. Prisoners in these camps were starved, beaten, shot, gassed, and used as subjects in grotesque medical experiments. Many thousands were forced at gunpoint to dig their own graves and then shot and unceremoniously dumped into them or sometimes even buried alive.

At first, though, humiliation was a favorite tactic used against imprisoned Jews. Abraham, a rabbi, was incarcerated in Papenburg in the fall of 1933. During his incarceration the rabbi attempted to meet the religious needs of his fellow prisoners by holding Jewish services during Rosh Hashanah, the Jewish New Year.

> The first day of the holiday: at six o'clock in the morning, we Jews who were newcomers in the camp were assigned to a special detachment. We were chased across the yard at a quick marching tempo. We were ordered to stop in front of a manure pit. We had climbed down into the pit and got into formation at the bottom. I was yanked out of the line of my comrades and positioned in the middle of the pit. [An SS officer] screamed at me, "Here you go, Rabbi. You can hold services here!" Everything in me rebelled against dragging our religion—so literally—into the dirt. I remained silent.[32]

The SS officer demanded to know whether the rabbi intended to refuse the order to lead Rosh Hashanah services in the manure pit. "I'm not holding services in a manure pit!" Abraham told him. The SS officer ordered the guards to pull Abraham out of the pit. "Rubber batons and gun butts rained down on me," Abraham said. "I was brought to my bunk unconscious. I lay there for two hours before regaining consciousness."[33]

Cruel Conditions at Home

Nazi brutality unquestionably reached its height in the camps, but Jews in the cities experienced other insults and misery on a daily basis. In schools Jewish children were bullied by classmates, while teachers were ordered

In Their Own Words

Jewish Children—Enemies of the State

John Silbermann attended school in Berlin in the 1930s. Silbermann says that as a young German Jew, he and other Jewish students were often bullied by their German classmates. He recalls the fear that filled his school days:

> I was only seven years of age in 1933 and I had just started school the year before. There were warnings from parents and others not to get mixed up in fights with the [German boys who were encouraged to abuse Jews]. . . . Jews were to be chased and beaten up. After 1933 it was just accepted that if you were a Jewish child you were liable to [be] beaten up, bullied or whatever else they chose to do with you. It was no use appealing to policemen or teachers because they're not supposed to interfere or even be interested in helping you because you are perceived as an enemy of the state. That was fed into my mind as a matter of self-preservation. One took care traveling to . . . school on the public trains. We used to travel in groups of twos and threes together, which gave a certain amount of protection. . . .
>
> The bullying and verbal assault was not confined to German children. It was quite common if some adult, who was nothing more than an ignorant thug, called you names, or kicked you. It was bullying all down the line and that was totally accepted.

Quoted in Jon E. Lewis, *Voices from the Holocaust*, e-book. London: Constable & Robinson, 2012.

not to protect the tyrannized youths. Teachers were encouraged to intimidate their Jewish students with the aim of getting them to drop out of school. Jewish children were routinely given poor grades, regardless of the quality of their work. One thirteen-year-old Jewish girl from the small town of Ostwestfalen-Lippe found herself attending a school assembly in which a teacher led a song that included anti-Semitic lyrics. "I was blind with rage and fear," the girl said. "I got up and decided . . . I'm not listening to this. I was pretty certain that they would kill me, grab me and break my bones. . . . But no one touched me. Somehow, the teachers as well as the pupils must have respected my courage. In a German school where discipline was stressed, to get up in the middle of a ceremony and leave without permission, that was incredible."[34]

Starting in 1933 the Nazis instituted a number of laws stripping Jews of their rights: Such laws prohibited Jews from owning land, barred them from employment in German-owned businesses, prohibited the exhibition of art by Jews in German museums, stripped Jewish immigrants from Poland of their German citizenship, and barred Jews from editing newspapers and teaching in schools. Hanna Bergas, a Jewish teacher, recalls the day in 1933 when she lost her job:

> The principal . . . stopped me, and asked me to come to his room.
> . . . When we were seated, he said, in a serious, embarrassed tone
> of voice, he had orders to ask me not to go into my classroom. I
> probably knew, he said, that I was not permitted to teach anymore
> at a German school. I did know, but was it to happen so abruptly?
> . . . I collected myself [and] my belongings. . . . In the afternoon
> . . . colleagues, pupils, their mothers came, some in a sad mood,
> others angry with their country, lovely bouquets of flowers, large
> and small, in their arms. In the evening, the little house was full of
> fragrance and colors, like for a funeral, I thought; and indeed, this
> was the funeral of my time teaching at a German public school.[35]

Aryanization

The most severe laws passed against the Jews were adopted by the *Reichstäg* in 1935. The so-called Nuremberg Laws specifically defined Jews and stripped them of their German citizenship. Under the Nuremberg Laws, anybody with at least three Jewish grandparents was declared a Jew. Former Jews who converted to Christianity were regarded as Jews.

The Nuremberg Laws prohibited Jews from marrying non-Jews. The Nuremberg Laws now cleared the way for Jews to be cast as outlaws in their own country. Whatever rights they had remaining were stripped.

Thus began a program of arresting Jews and deporting them to Poland and other occupied countries, where they lived in ghettos—typically, lowly neighborhoods where they were forced to live in ramshackle dwellings. From time to time SS troops cleaned out the ghettos, arresting Jews and sending them to concentration camps. As the Jews were deported from Germany, they were forced to leave behind most of their possessions. This included their homes and life savings as well as clothing, furnishings, and other household goods. The seizure of Jewish assets was known as Aryanization.

> **WORDS IN CONTEXT**
> **Aryanization**
> The forced transfer of Jewish-owned property to German ownership.

These assets were taken by the Nazi government but also by unscrupulous Germans who paid the Jews pennies for their homes and possessions, promising to help them escape to other countries. In most cases the Jews were duped: They lost their homes and money and were shipped to overcrowded ghettos in Poland and other countries, and eventually to concentration camps.

After the German invasion of Poland in September 1939 many of the Polish communities along the German border were absorbed into Germany. One such town was Sosnowiec, where Bella Jakubowicz's father owned a knitting mill. First, the Nazis seized the mill. And then Bella's family lost all of their personal possessions. She says,

> In the fall of 1939, there was a knock on our door. And there was a German woman, and two SS men were with her and . . . they came into our apartment, and she walked through the apartment and she turned to the SS men and she said, "*Ich hab'es gerne.*

Alles." [which means] "I like it. All of it." And they sent in some people a day later . . . they brought in a truck and they . . . took everything out of our house. . . . All our furniture, rugs, whatever she wanted. [In return] she sent us an old table, some chairs,

Jewish women from Germany cook in buckets outside the stables where they lived after being deported to Poland in 1938. Deported Jews endured squalid conditions in the ghettos of Poland and other Nazi-occupied lands.

some old beds . . . a wardrobe, probably what she had. She must not have been a very well-to-do woman, but you see she became rich, because she was German."[36]

Yellow Stars

Losing their property was a devastating blow to the Jews of Germany, but the Nazis had other humiliations in store for them. In September 1941 the *Reichstäg* enacted a law requiring Jews to wear the six-pointed Star of David sewn into their clothes with the word *Jude* (Jew) stitched crudely across the star. The star, yellow and about the size of a human palm, had to be sewn breast-high over the heart. By wearing the star on their outer garments, Jews could be identified by shopkeepers, landlords, and others who were now by law forbidden to grant them service. Moreover, since they were easily identifiable, Jews were open to abuse and attacks on the streets by Nazi thugs. Elisabeth Freund, a Jewish woman from Berlin, relates the treatment she received in public once she started wearing the star: "Sometimes guttersnipes call out abusive words after me. And occasionally Jews are said to have been beaten up. Someone tells me of an experience in the city train. A mother saw that her little girl was sitting beside a Jew: 'Lieschen, sit down on the other bench, you don't need to sit beside a Jew.'"[37]

> **WORDS IN CONTEXT**
> *Jude*
> The German word for *Jew*.

Nazi law also included this humiliation: All women had to include the middle name "Sarah" in their signatures—a reference to the wife of Abraham whose teachings, according to the holy scriptures, led to the founding of Judaism. Erich Hopp says Jewish women could be arrested if they failed to include Sarah in their signatures. While living underground the Hopps received aid from a Dr. Beier, an art historian in the city of Potsdam whose wife was a friend of Hopp's wife, Charlotte. Beier's wife, who was Jewish, returned to Germany in 1942 after spending several years on the island of Crete in the Mediterranean Sea. "*Frau* Beier was later sent to a concentration

*In 1941 German lawmakers ordered Jews to wear the six-pointed Star of David sewn into their clothes with the word **Jude** (Jew) stitched crudely across the star. The star made it easy for shopkeepers and others to identify Jews and refuse them services.*

camp because having just returned from Crete, she did not know of the Nazi rule that all Jewish women must sign with the middle name 'Sarah.'" Hopp says. "She died, worn out, shortly after liberation."[38]

Germans Helping Jews

As Hopp's story illustrates, a few Germans found sympathy for Jews and helped where they could. Such help was provided secretly and usually for close friends or relatives—for if the government learned that German citizens were helping Jews, they could face severe consequences. Germans found to be aiding Jews were often sent to concentration camps.

Nevertheless, some Germans risked their lives to help Jewish friends. Erna Puterman found refuge in a friend's apartment for many years—until the end of World War II. In 1942 the Jewish woman knocked on a friend's door and said, "Today they took my mother." The friend replied, "Then you stay here."[39] Another woman, Irma Simon, hastily packed a suitcase and left her apartment when she learned Gestapo agents were on their way to her home. As she struggled down a Berlin street with the heavy suitcase, a German shoemaker—whom she did not know—emerged from his shop and carried her suitcase back in. The shoemaker and his brother hid Simon, her husband, and their son in their apartments until the war's end.

Stealing Eggs

Other Jews who could not find help from Germans were forced to go underground, fending for themselves. They tore the Star of David off their clothes and wandered the cities, spending their days in public cafés trying to blend in with other Germans. At night they slept in parks or train stations. Food was scarce. To buy food they needed to show their identification papers to shop owners who, under law, were prohibited from selling food to Jews. In most cities, though, some Jews could make connections through black markets where they were able to obtain forged identification papers.

But most Jews simply went hungry, eating only when they could steal food. Blanca Rosenberg, a Jewish woman, obtained phony identification papers and was able to find a job as a maid for a German family. Rosenberg was told by her employer that her food ration consisted of one small loaf of bread per day. "Stupefied by the ration," Rosenberg recalled, "I turned to Cesia (the maid she was replacing) and said, 'How do you manage on this ration?' She smiled, 'Look, you're the cook, so fill up on the soup you're making.'"[40]

The German woman for whom Rosenberg worked kept a close eye on the fruit trees in the backyard. Rosenberg knew then that she could not steal fruit from the trees. But she did slip an egg out from beneath the hen from time to time—even eating the eggs raw. "Unlike the fruit trees, the chickens never gave me away,"[41] Rosenberg says.

Other Jews were not as fortunate as Rosenberg. Hopp and his family lived underground until the end of the war. The Hopps ate sporadically, consuming whatever food they could find—on occasion horse meat that Hopp butchered himself. "While cutting horse meat . . . I cut my finger," Hopp says. "The meat was no longer fresh, and I immediately developed a serious infection. I ran a high fever, and pain tortured me day and night. I thought that my last day had come and instructed [my son] Wolfgang, if I died, to empty my pockets and take my body into the woods. But after three months' illness I was again quite well."[42]

Night of the Broken Glass

For the Hopps and other Jews it seemed as though conditions in Germany could not grow worse. But they were wrong: The night of November 9, 1938, marked a change in the German government's policy against the Jews from one of persecution to one of extermination. Two days earlier an incident occurred in Paris, France, that led to the virtual destruction of German Jewry. To protest against the German government's treatment of Jews, Herschel Grynszpan, a German-born Jew who had fled to Paris, assassinated German diplomat Ernst vom Rath while Rath visited France.

Goebbels's propaganda machine declared that Grynszpan was part of a worldwide Jewish conspiracy to destroy the German state, stoking fears among the German people. On the night of November 9 Nazi thugs ran amok in the streets of cities in Germany as well as the Nazi-occupied countries of Austria and Czechoslovakia, vandalizing Jewish homes, Jewish-owned businesses, and synagogues. They smashed windows and set buildings on fire. This sad chapter in German history is known as *Kristallnacht* (Night of the Broken Glass).

Hermann Gottfried, a Berlin Jew, was sixteen years old on *Kristallnacht*. He said his apartment was broken into that night by thugs who not only vandalized his home but also stole from his family. "It was

Looking Back

The Swift Campaign of Persecution

Marion A. Kaplan, professor of Hebrew and Judaic Studies at Columbia University in New York, says the Nazi campaign of persecution against the Jews occurred so quickly that many Jews found themselves confused and unsure how to react. Jews who had lived in Germany their whole lives were, within the space of five years, turned into their nation's enemies—a hard fact for many to accept given they had considered themselves loyal Germans. She says,

> What is striking in the victims' accounts is not whether the Nazis intended the destruction of the Jews due to their unmitigated and unparalleled hatred or whether they backed into it, but the speed and the ambiguities of the attack against Jewish life, and the speed and the ambivalences with which the Jews reacted in the years before 1938. In 1933, a Jewish ten-year-old observed Nazis marching with placards reading "Germans, Don't Buy From Jews. World Jewry Wants to Destroy Germany. Defend Yourselves." But in 1935, her father was still decorated for active service in the past war, receiving a citation signed by Berlin's chief of police. Jews read these mixed messages with fear and hope. They thought about and prepared for emigration, all the while wishing they would not have to leave their homeland.

Marion A. Kaplan, *Between Dignity and Despair: Jewish Life in Nazi Germany.* New York: Oxford University Press, 1998, p. 4.

the neighbors who came into the apartment and smashed the glass and smashed the china and took whatever they wanted," he said. "It was a mixture of SS guys and neighbors. People saw an opportunity to get things that they didn't have."[43]

Armin Hertz was fifteen years old during *Kristallnacht*. His parents owned a shop that was ransacked that ill-fated night. Even with danger in the streets, Hertz says, his mother worried about her sister and her two children and sent him to see whether they were safe. Hertz rode his bicycle to his aunt's neighborhood—which he found in chaos:

> I saw all the stores destroyed, windows broken, everything lying in the street. They were even going into the stores and running away with the merchandise. Finally I got to my aunt's house and I saw a large crowd assembled in front of the store. The fire department was there; the police were there. The fire department was pouring water on the adjacent building. The synagogue in the back was on fire, but they were not putting the water on the synagogue. The police were there watching it. I mingled with the crowd. I didn't want to be too obvious. I didn't want to get into trouble. But I heard from people talking that the people who live there were all evacuated, all safe in the neighborhood with friends. So I went right back and reported to my mother.[44]

The Nazi campaign against the Jews was nothing less than an attempt to eradicate an entire ethnic group. The fact that so many ordinary German citizens participated in the persecution of the Jews—either smashing the glass in Jewish homes or shops, cheating Jews out of their homes and savings, or looking the other way when a Jewish child was assaulted by bullies—remains a black mark on German history that may never be wiped away.

Chapter Four

To Be Young in Nazi Germany

As a public school dropout, Adolf Hitler held much contempt for formal education and had little faith in the German schools to indoctrinate young people into the principles of National Socialism. Instead, Hitler intended to make use of the widely popular youth organizations in Germany, of which there were hundreds. An umbrella group, the *Reich* Committee of German Youth Associations, oversaw these groups, the total membership of which numbered more than 10 million. These groups were not unlike the youth organizations found in America at the time, such as the Boy Scouts, Pop Warner Football, or church-sponsored groups such as the Catholic Youth Organization. Some of the youth groups in Germany were sports-oriented, some dedicated to public service, and some to outdoor life.

By the time Hitler ascended to the chancellorship, one of the smallest youth associations in Germany was the *Hitler-Jugend* (Hitler Youth), which totaled just some one hundred thousand members nationwide. The Hitler Youth, created in 1926 by the Nazi Party, was dedicated to indoctrinating young people into the principles of National Socialism.

> **WORDS IN CONTEXT**
> *Hitler-Jugend*
> Hitler Youth; an organization used for indoctrinating young people into Nazi ideology and preparing boys for military service.

Hitler Youth members played soccer and went camping, but they also sat through lectures and speeches extolling the virtues of German supremacy. They listened to their leaders rail against Jews. They were taught to worship Hitler. And they also learned how to march and salute and use weapons. After passing a series of tests, proving his or her devotion to the cause, a young person received a special gift—a symbol of the Nazi state: a dagger.

Test of Courage

Alfons Heck received his dagger shortly after his tenth birthday. Heck grew up in the small town of Wittlich near the German border with Luxembourg. Born in 1929, at the age of nine Heck entered the *Jungvolk* (German Youth)—a division of the Hitler Youth established for the youngest members. Recalls Heck:

> It would be a fallacy to assume that we joined simply to serve the Fatherland. Such sentiments only came to the fore at special occasions, like induction ceremonies, flag consecrations and as a part of the many boring speeches we had to endure. Like most 10-year-olds, I craved action, and the Hitler Youth had that in abundance. Far from being forced to enter the ranks of the *Jungvolk*, I could barely contain my impatience and was, in fact, accepted before I was quite 10. It seemed like an exciting life, free from parental supervision, filled with "duties" that seemed sheer pleasure. Precision marching was something one could endure for hiking, camping, war games in the field, and a constant emphasis on sports. . . .
>
> There were the paraphernalia and the symbols, the pomp and mysticism, very close in feeling to religious rituals. One of the first significant demands was the so-called *Mutprobe*: "test of courage," which was usually administered after a six-month period of probation. The members of my *Schar*, a platoon-like unit of about 40–50 boys, were required to dive off the three-meter board—about 10 feet high—head first into the town's swimming pool. There were some stinging belly flops but the pain was worth it when our *Fähnleinführer*, the 15-year-old leader of our *Fähnlein*, (literally 'little flag') a company-like unit of about 160 boys, handed us the coveted dagger with its description *Blood and Honor*. From that moment on we were fully accepted.[45]

Von Schirach's Mission

To administer the youth programs in Germany, Hitler appointed a dedicated follower, Baldur von Schirach. He was assigned the task of taking control of the various youth organizations and remaking them into groups that adhered to the same mission as the Hitler Youth: to make young people into dedicated Nazis. Hitler believed the job so important that he made von Schirach a top deputy, answerable to no one else in the Nazi hierarchy.

Von Schirach was a most unlikely Nazi. His mother was an American, having been born in Philadelphia. Moreover, von Schirach was descended from two signers of the Declaration of Independence: Arthur Middleton and Thomas Heyward Jr., both of South Carolina. Nevertheless, von Schirach joined the Nazi Party in 1924 at the age of seventeen and in 1933 was appointed by Hitler as Youth Leader of the German *Reich*.

> **WORDS IN CONTEXT**
> *Mutprobe*
> A test of courage usually administered after a six-month period of probation in the Hitler Youth.

It turned out to be a formidable task—there were hundreds of groups, each with their own leaders, some of whom were dedicated Nazis, some of whom were not. For three years von Schirach sacked leaders, found others to head the organizations, rewrote their bylaws, and then in 1936 completed his mission by convincing Hitler to outlaw all youth organizations—with the exception of the Hitler Youth. On December 1, 1936, Hitler issued this decree: "All of the German youth in the Reich is organized within the Hitler Youth. The German youth, besides being reared within the family and schools, shall be educated physically, intellectually and morally in the spirit of National Socialism . . . through the Hitler Youth."[46]

By March 1939, when it was evident that Germany would soon enter the battlefield against its neighbors, the Führer saw the Hitler Youth as a valuable tool for preparing young men and women for the coming war. At that time, membership in the Hitler Youth numbered some 7 million young Germans. The government estimated that about 4 million young people were not members. And so that month the government made membership in the Hitler Youth mandatory.

Members of the Hitler Youth take part in a parade around 1936. The Hitler Youth indoctrinated young people into the principles of National Socialism; those who showed dedication to the cause were singled out for leadership posts.

Biking, Boating, and Camping

Prior to 1939 young people who voluntarily joined the Hitler Youth typically became members at the age of six or seven and remained in the organization until the age of eighteen. Both boys and girls were eligible to join. Certainly, the Hitler Youth engaged in activities that young people could enjoy. Boys and girls went biking, boating, and camping. They learned how to swim, ski, and play soccer. They took field trips to museums and zoos. Some Hitler Youth units formed choirs, orchestras, and marching bands. Hitler Youth members were issued uniforms, which they wore proudly as they marched in parades.

To top Nazi leaders, though, the Hitler Youth served a much more important purpose than simply providing opportunities to visit zoos or learn how to ski. Nazi leaders looked upon the Hitler Youth as a vehicle for introducing boys and girls into the principles of National Socialism. Upon joining, each child was issued a performance book in which Hitler Youth leaders made notes on the young person's progress. Children whose performance books included glowing comments about their dedication to National Socialism were singled out for leadership posts in the Hitler Youth. Herbert Lutz, whose father held a leadership post in the Cologne Nazi Party, says he joined the Hitler Youth in 1935, at the age of seven. Nazi ideology stressed discipline and respect for leadership. According to Lutz, these lessons were taught in the Hitler Youth:

> **WORDS IN CONTEXT**
> **performance book**
> A notebook that charted the path toward acceptance of Nazism by Hitler Youth members.

> The discipline in the Hitler Youth was maintained simply by having certain punishments. For instance, if you talked out of turn, you were punished by not being allowed to wear your [uniform] scarf for three weeks. That was not for really severe crimes; it was for clowning around or whatever. The other punishment was a more severe punishment. Part of our uniform was a dagger. Can you imagine a ten-year-old carrying a dagger? It was an honor to be allowed to wear that. If you did something really nasty, you were not allowed to wear your scarf and your dagger and that meant that you were an outcast.[47]

At the age of ten, after three or four years of indoctrination into National Socialism, Hitler Youth members were expected to recite this oath, while standing beneath the Nazi flag: "I promise in the Hitler Youth to do my duty at all times in love and faithfulness to help the Führer— so help me God."[48] According to Heck the oath was intended to make Hitler Youth members believe they were the Führer's close allies in his mission to spread Nazism across Germany and the rest of Europe. Says Heck, "Adolf Hitler ceaselessly encouraged the feeling that we were his trusted helpers and used it with brilliant intuition."[49]

Rifles and Rucksacks

After taking the oath, Hitler Youth members moved on to activities resembling those found on military bases. They were issued rifles and rucksacks and required to drill and participate in mock battles. "Sometimes when we had Hitler Youth meetings in the early days we did these so-called military drills," says Lutz.

> I found them boring. I had done that a thousand times. . . . Then again, I learned how to circumvent certain inconveniences by, for instance, volunteering for training in the signal corps. I learned Morse code. To [Nazi officials] it was cheap military training. When we were drafted eventually, some of us knew how to fly an airplane, some of us knew how to operate radio equipment. But, to us kids, working with real military transmitters and using Morse code and being up there right with the big shots in the military made us feel good. It made us feel important.[50]

Still, the training could be rigorous. Army officers oversaw the boys' training in the field. Heinz Müller, from the town of Duisberg and once a Hitler Youth member, related that the officer in charge of his training greeted new arrivals at camp by first ordering them to lie facedown in the mud and do push-ups. As the boys lowered their bodies into the mud, the officer stepped on their backs, pushing them farther into the muck. According to Müller, the officers played games with the boys—for example, asking for volunteers to help with clerical work. Boys who raised their hands instead found themselves assigned to latrine duty. Nevertheless,

In Their Own Words

Hitler's Eyes

In 1942 eight-year-old Karen Finell joined the *Jungmädelbund* and attended a Nazi rally in Berlin. Finell describes the adoration showered on Hitler and her own personal feelings when she caught the attention of the Führer:

> Everyone was standing, waiting for the Führer. Speeches were made, and we continued to wait as the sun rose higher, blasting down on us. After a long time, a rumor went through the aisles: he had arrived. Our arms and hands stretched out in the expected "Heil Hitler" salute. . . . Teachers watched to make sure that we stood rigid, at attention with our arms outstretched. I felt my body turning numb and I could not even move my legs. Sweat dripped over my eyebrows, burning my eyes. I am not a weakling, I am a strong German girl, I told myself, as my arm lost all feeling.
>
> Suddenly a roar filled the stadium. It started in the rear and moved forward like the salvo of drums, growing loud and louder until it was deafening. A chorus of voices screamed, *"Sieg Heil! Sieg Heil! Sieg Heil!"*
>
> There *he* was. . . . Then, at the moment when his car passed the row where I stood . . . his head turned to the left, and his eyes, for the briefest moment in time, met mine. They were such a deep blue, the color of Mother's sapphire ring, hard, like a faceted stone and just as fiery. Never again have I encountered anyone with eyes that color, eyes that I would never forget.

Karen Finell, *Good-bye to the Mermaids: A Childhood Lost in Hitler's Berlin*. Columbia: University of Missouri Press, 2006, pp. 66–67.

Müller said, all boys learned how to use weapons, including rifles, hand grenades, and machine guns.

Hitler Youth Girls

While the boys were learning to use weapons or operate military radios, girls who joined the Hitler Youth were directed toward a much different path. Young girls were expected to join the *Jungmädelbund* (Young Girls' League). At the age of fourteen they moved on to the *Bund Deutscher Mädel* (League of German Girls). As with the boys, the girls participated in

Girls, who also joined the Hitler Youth, attend a rally around 1934. The organization taught girls to be loyal, obedient, and devoted wives and mothers—in line with expectations of women in Nazi society.

sports, went on field trips, and camped out. But during their time together the girls were taught the values expected of women in the Nazi society: to be loyal and obedient wives, to produce children for the *Reich*, and to be capable and dedicated homemakers for their husbands and children.

Ursula Mahlendorf, whose father joined the SS, was an enthusiastic member who rose to a leadership position in the League of German Girls. "I always knew that I participated in Hitler Youth with greater enthusiasm than my classmates," she said. "I now understand some of the reasons for this: my father, before he died in 1939, had become a member of the SS. After Father's death, Hitler gradually became an idealized substitute father for me. I championed Hitler's cause."[51]

Belief and Beauty

When girls turned eighteen they were no longer required to participate in Hitler Youth activities. By that age, Nazi officials hoped, the girls would find proper Aryan husbands. However, young women between the ages of eighteen and twenty-one had the opportunity to join the *Glaube und Schönheit* (Belief and Beauty Society). On the surface, membership in the Belief and Beauty Society offered the participants training in a profession—but the training was limited to the types of jobs Nazi officials believed young women should pursue. By attending Belief and Beauty meetings young women learned such skills as sewing, weaving, cooking, baking, ironing, and child rearing. "We did a lot of weaving in our [Belief and Beauty] schools . . . so that this old craft could be kept alive or reintroduced," says Hannelore Canzler, who had been a member of a Belief and Beauty Society. "It was all part of Personal Life Skills, even the furnishings in one's home. We shouldn't just senselessly put modern industrial furniture in our homes later on, but rather be careful to get useful ones."[52]

Canzler also attended the Healthy Life Choices classes in the Belief and Beauty Society: "It included the areas [of] healthy eating, such as vitamin-rich cooking; but also healthcare, nursing, and baby care. A lot of time was spent on healthy living in general. That's why we said, 'We don't smoke, we don't drink, and we use makeup sparingly'—just enough for the skin to still breathe underneath. We swim a lot, and we place importance in good posture when standing or walking."[53]

There were recreational activities for members of the Belief and Beauty Society: Some groups offered participants training in physical education and sports such as gymnastics, horseback riding, pistol shooting, and fencing. Belief and Beauty societies also stressed painting, sculpture, and fashion design.

Even in the Belief and Beauty organizations, though, members could find something of a military element. Belief and Beauty members wore uniforms—dark blue jackets, white blouses, and dark blue hats and coats. In the summer the blue jackets were replaced by white blazers. On their uniforms the girls wore patches awarded for skill in particular subjects or designating them as leaders.

Labor Service

Upon reaching the age of eighteen, both males and females were expected to join the *Reichsarbeitsdienst* (Labor Service). Labor Service duty lasted six months. Male Labor Service members helped build roads, lay railroad tracks, construct dikes, fill swamps, and complete other projects requiring hard and heavy work. Upon joining the Labor Service, a young German man was issued a shovel and bicycle and each morning, upon arriving for duty, was told where his labor was needed. At the conclusion of the young man's commitment to the Labor Service, he was conscripted into the German army. Young women were assigned to Labor Service chores as well—although the work was less physically taxing. Girls were often assigned to help farmers in fields or farmwives with household chores.

> **WORDS IN CONTEXT**
> *Reichsarbeitsdienst*
> Labor Service; a national system employed to make use of young people's labor in public works projects.

William Shirer said he often encountered young men and women in the Labor Service at work as he traveled across Germany during the 1930s. Says Shirer, "In most cases it did no harm to a city boy and girl to spend six months in the compulsory Labor Service, where they lived

Young men in the Reichsarbeitsdienst *(Reich Labor Service) work on a construction project in 1937. Male Labor Service members were issued a shovel and bicycle and given their assignments when they arrived for duty each morning.*

outdoors and learned the value of manual labor and of getting along with those of different backgrounds. No one who traveled up and down Germany in those days and talked with the young in their camps and watched them work and play and sing could fail to see that, however sinister the teaching, here was an incredibly dynamic youth movement."[54]

Building the Master Race

Author and historian Dagmar Reese points out that despite their insistence that Aryans were members of a "master race," it took the Nazis considerable time and effort to transform young Germans into the Nazi ideal of a perfect human specimen. That is why the Nazis insisted young people be shielded from books and other media that offered contrary views of Nazism. The League of German Girls, Reese says, was an important component in ensuring girls grew up to be dedicated Nazis:

> Contrary to what one would expect, the Aryan required an unprecedented degree of . . . influence in order to unfold his or her natural superiority. The members of the master race were surrounded by an entire web of specially created organizations; these enveloped all their activities, shaping the phases of their lives. In the bosom of the League of German Girls, views about how to educate a German girl and mold her into a proper German woman took on concrete, palpable form. . . .
>
> The path of education of a German girl had to be as uniform as her external appearance. Next to the parental home and the school, the League of German Girls was considered the third educational institution in society. It was responsible for educating female German youth . . . in the spirit of National Socialism, dedicated to service to its people and the folk community. How this external National Socialist education of girls was to be organized and implemented . . . was set down in precise detail.

Dagmar Reese, *Growing Up Female in Nazi Germany*. Ann Arbor: University of Michigan Press, 2006, pp. 21–22.

Nazifying the Schools

Admission into the Labor Service or the Belief and Beauty Society followed completion of a young person's formal education. Although Hitler placed more importance on the Hitler Youth to indoctrinate young people into the world of National Socialism, the schools were Nazified as well. Soon after ascending to the chancellorship, Hitler appointed a close ally—Bernhard Rust, a fanatical Nazi and unemployed schoolmaster—as minister of Science, Education, and Popular Culture. (Three years earlier school officials in the city of Hanover had sacked Rust, alleging that he maintained a romantic relationship with a student.) In his new position Rust ordered all textbooks replaced with new textbooks that reflected Nazi ideology. Teachers regarded as less than dedicated Nazis were fired. Every teacher was expected to join the National Socialist Teachers' League which, under German law, was dedicated to extolling the principles of National Socialism.

These new textbooks falsified history and the sciences. Biology classes, for example, taught that Germans were members of a master race and all other peoples were physically and intellectually inferior. Jews were singled out as subhuman. German history was rewritten, suggesting that the German people had overcome centuries of struggle to take their places as leaders of the world. Advances in mathematics and physics pioneered by Jewish scientists, such as Albert Einstein, were ignored. Alice Hamilton, an American physician traveling in Germany in 1933, observed the state of education in the German schools. She says, "The most important subject in the new curriculum is history, with the emphasis laid on German heroes, German inventors, German rulers, poets, artists. The German child must be taught that his nation is superior to every other in every field."[55]

Even the youngest students were indoctrinated into the principles of National Socialism and taught to worship their Führer. The text of the storybook titled *The Führer Comes* illustrates how young children were first exposed to Nazism:

> Today Klaus' mother does not need to wake him. He springs from bed on his own. Today is an important holiday. From the window the Swastika flags wave. . . . In the shop windows stand pictures of the Führer. . . . The boys climb up trees. . . . When a

flag-bearer passes, Klaus raises his right arm in salute. All at once Klaus hears Heil salutes from afar. The shouts sound even nearer, and then Klaus sees the Führer. He stands in the car and waves in a friendly manner. Heil! Heil! calls Klaus as loud as he can. What a pity, the Führer is already past! But Klaus continually calls: Heil Hitler! Heil Hitler![56]

The Value of the Young

As the story of Klaus illustrates, Hitler knew the value of young people to the future of the *Reich*. He knew that he had to indoctrinate them into the principles of National Socialism at an early age so that they would grow up to be dedicated Nazis. He chose not to rely solely on the schools to accomplish this aim but to use young people's leisure time for this purpose as well. That is why he placed so much importance on the Hitler Youth, and why Hitler regarded von Schirach's job with such a degree of importance that he made his director of youth programs answerable only to the Führer. For as Hitler made plans to wage war across Europe, he knew his army would rely on a military composed of young, able, and dedicated Nazis willing to sacrifice their lives for the cause of National Socialism.

Chapter Five

Life on the Home Front

Thirteen-year-old Ilse Hertzstell was struck by the reality of what the coming war would be like for the people of Germany on August 28, 1939. On that day Hertzstell's family—and all other citizens of Germany—were issued ration cards. Germans were required to take their ration cards to the food markets and other stores. Their cards were marked each time they made purchases, and their purchases were limited—rationed—to help ensure there would be no shortages of food and other basic necessities.

"Main food (meat, lard, coffee and sugar) could only be obtained by using ration cards," Hertzstell recalls. "From September 25 of that year, bread and eggs were also rationed. The Nazi officials hoped to prevent famine such as seen in World War I by starting this rationing well in advance. . . . Shortly after the war started most all food products with the exception of potatoes and vegetables were rationed. Only minimum amounts were to be had. A short time after the food rationing went into effect, coupons were issued for clothes, shoes and many household items. All of this occurred on November 12, 1939."[57]

Three days after Hertzstell's family was issued its ration card, 1.5 million German troops crossed the border into Poland, touching off World War II. Adolf Hitler set his plan into motion to dominate the European continent. German troops launched a relentless campaign against the ill-prepared Polish army. Two days later England and France declared war on Germany, dedicating themselves to halting German aggression. Soon the entire European continent was engulfed in a war that eventually spread to virtually every corner of the planet.

Hunger on the Home Front

Despite the issuance of the ration cards, hunger soon became a hard fact of life for the German people. Much of the food grown on German farms and in the German-occupied countries was diverted to the military, leaving less for people at home. Trains, trucks, and other modes of transporting food were also taken over by the military, further reducing food supplies to civilians.

Moreover, in the years prior to the invasion of Poland, the Nazi government poured its resources into building arms rather than stockpiling food. By early 1941 signs of hunger in Germany had become clear to international observers. "We know that there is rationing of extreme severity in Germany now . . . the huge rearmament program has brought serious want and malnutrition to the German masses even before the war had begun,"[58] wrote Calvin B. Hoover, a member of the Council of National Defense, an agency established by the US government to prepare America for entry into the war.

In 1941—two years after Germany attacked Poland—Hoover made the observation that there were few dogs in Germany, giving rise to his suspicion that people were eating their pets. He wrote, "Dogs [have] almost disappeared in the stew pots [presenting] a general picture of near starvation."[59]

A year later Mildred Fish Harnack reported that her cupboard was habitually short of food. An American, she met her husband, German student Arvid Harnack, while both were studying at the University of Wisconsin. In 1929 Mildred and Arvid returned to Germany where Arvid accepted a post as a professor at the University of Berlin. When war was declared in 1939 Mildred and her husband were trapped in Germany, unable to return to America. In late 1942 she wrote her mother-in-law, who lived in the city of Darmstadt in southern Germany, that she and Arvid were living on little more than potatoes and other scraps of food they could manage to find. "Could you send us [more] potatoes?" she wrote in a letter to Arvid's mother. "We eat potatoes now each evening. This evening we had a costly small potato. . . . We scrape together radishes with salt and a salad from parsley root."[60]

German soldiers on the Eastern Front line up for meals at a field kitchen in the early 1940s. Much of the food grown on German farms and in occupied lands was diverted to the military, creating shortages for German civilians.

Lack of Consumer Goods

During the war years new clothing was also hard to come by in Germany. As with food, the raw materials to make fabric were diverted first to military use. In addition, a coal shortage in Germany meant many nonessential factories—those that did not produce arms and ammunition—had to be shut down for lack of fuel. Among the factories considered nonessential were those that produced textiles.

Shoes were also in short supply because leather was diverted to military use as well—troops needed new boots, particularly the soldiers on the Eastern Front where the snow was deep and winters brutally cold. As a result, many people in the German cities had to make do with old clothes and shoes that they continually had to patch and repair.

The Allies had a hand in making sure the basic necessities of life were in short supply in Germany. Starting in 1940 the British Royal Air Force (RAF) commenced a relentless bombing campaign of German cities, targeting factories as a way of crippling Germany's ability to resupply its troops with fresh arms and supplies. A 1945 report prepared by the US Senate Committee on Military Affairs said the bombing campaign had a direct impact on the supplies of food, new clothes, and shoes, as well as coal to heat people's homes. The committee's report said that prior to the 1939 invasion of Poland consumer goods in Germany were generally available. However, the report continues,

The day war broke out the situation changed radically. Food and soap were rationed immediately; textiles, footwear, and fuel shortly thereafter; 1942 marked a new stage in German rationing. There was marked deterioration in the supply of consumer goods and services to civilians. Production was slowed up and valuable stocks destroyed by the air war. The wholesale destruction of dwellings vastly increase the demand for household furniture, clothing, and textiles. . . .

The clothing ration deteriorated constantly. . . . The clothing ration for most articles was suspended for all non-priority adults [those who were not members of the military]. There was a similar development in various categories of household goods. With intensified war the sale of household articles to other than air-raid victims and the war-disabled was frequently suspended in the raided districts and cut to a minimum in the rest of the country. . . .

The extreme shortage of leather made special difficulties for footwear. By the end of 1943 one serviceable pair of shoes made it impossible to obtain a permit [to purchase new shoes].[61]

Nights Without Light

Hunger and shortages of clothing and shoes may have been slowly taking its toll on German morale, but many German citizens also found themselves in danger of perishing with little or no warning. The Allied bombers made danger a way of life. Each night German citizens were forced to take shelter in basements and other underground shelters, such as subway stations. They were ordered to extinguish all lights at night—these nights without light were known as *blackouts*. On the street level all lights had to be turned off to make it difficult for the Allied bombers to find targets. "Another change in our lifestyle occurred shortly after the war started, 'Total Blackout,'" says Hertzstell. "No light was allowed to come from any window, doorway or opening to the outside. An Air Raid Warden was assigned to each block. It was his duty to enforce the requirement that all rules concerning the Blackout were obeyed. Otherwise, one risked severe punishment. It was a requirement that everyone go immediately to their assigned shelter when the alarm sounded."[62]

> **WORDS IN CONTEXT**
> **blackout**
> Nighttime event in which residents of German cities were ordered by the government to extinguish all lights to prevent Allied bombers from spotting targets.

But the Allied bombing crews found ways to identify their targets—usually German factories—in missions designed to cripple the country's capacity to make weapons. Sibylle Sarah Niemoeller recalls the bombing crews dropping incendiary devices that lit up the sky over Berlin, providing the bombardiers with enough light to spot their targets. She was a teenager at the time and the daughter of an aristocratic family who lived in the Berlin suburb of Dahlem. "The pilots dropped luminous devices, appropriately named 'Christmas trees' by the Berliners, in order to illuminate the scene before unloading their [bombs],"[63] she says.

Sheltering from Air Raids

Bombings did not occur only at night—at any moment of the day the air raid sirens could blast as the sky filled with Allied bombers. Hertzstell recalls stepping off the train one morning at 8:30 a.m. on her way to work in a Berlin office building when the air raid sirens went off. "I just made it across the street into the shelter," she says.

We were in there for several hours. We could hear explosions all around us. At some point some firebombs fell on the house of the shelter we were in. The fires were soon put out. After the 'All Clear' siren I walked home with my heavy briefcase. It took about 25 minutes. The streetcars were still out of order. I could smell smoke and see fires and dust all around. It was the strangest looking sky. This was one of the worst raids on the southeast part of Berlin. Usually there were not that many raids during the day.

When [my sister] Lottie got home that afternoon, she told me all the terrible things that happened to her. Her office was only a half-block from our Aunt Trudchen and Uncle Paul's house. She had to walk around some dead people to check our relatives. All were okay, but their house was totally demolished. They had lost everything except what they had in the suitcases they had taken to the shelter with them."[64]

Inside the shelters the terror could drive city dwellers to near insanity. One Berliner describes what went through his mind as he waited out an air raid: "You have so much time here in the shelter to think, to imagine annihilations. . . . Choking, drowning, smashed, burning to death in a closed room, going crazy from fear under the rubble of a collapsed house, horrible injuries from shrapnel. . . . Torn off limbs with shredded organs and stomachs torn open by the air pressure from a bomb. . . . Your imagination goes nuts."[65]

And after the air raid, when the survivors emerged from their shelters many of them were ordered by the police to help gather corpses. Says one Berlin woman, "Ever since I was bombed out and had to help recover those buried under the rubble, I labor under a fear of death. The symptoms are always the same. First sweat on my scalp, then a boring in my

Soldiers and civilians clear rubble after an air raid in Germany in the mid-1940s. After air raids, police often ordered survivors to help gather corpses as well as clear rubble.

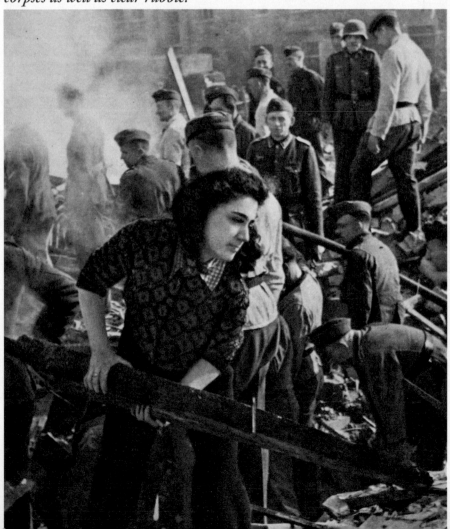

In Their Own Words

"They Even Closed the Candy Store"

Just sixteen years old when the war commenced, Sibylle Sarah Niemoeller recalls that in her home in the Berlin neighborhood of Dahlem, news of the attack on Poland was greeted with a sense of dread. Already, ration cards had been issued, and shortages of food were to become a way of life. But for a young girl in Nazi Germany, it was the loss of the neighborhood candy store that mostly illustrated what war would mean:

> I demanded to know what this would mean for our lives. After all, wars, as everybody knew, took place on battlefields and certainly not in the streets of Dahlem. My mother told me that there probably would be a blackout, and all young men would be inducted into the armed forces. Clothing and food would become scarce, with new ration cards each month or even each week for everything. . . . Surely not candy?

> Tearing my bicycle out of the garage, I raced to the store opposite the Dahlem Dorf subway station, where I came to a screeching halt. I noticed a sign on the door, scribbled with pencil on a piece of cardboard: closed for the duration of the war!

> For the duration of the war? Did this mean until the war was over? What if it lasted more than just a few days or weeks? Or even months? I just could not believe it; the unthinkable had happened. They even closed the candy store.

Sibylle Sarah Niemoeller, *Crowns, Crosses, and Stars: My Youth in Prussia, Surviving Hitler, and a Life Beyond*. West Lafayette, IN: Purdue University Press, 2012, p. 105.

spine, a catch in my throat, the roof of my mouth is parched, my heart pounds. . . . Only I could pray. The brain gropes for words."[66]

And a man from Hamburg says he could not perform the labors of carrying corpses while sober—he had to deaden his senses by gulping schnapps, a very strong German alcoholic beverage. He says,

> One must, especially if the corpses and body parts are already in a state of decay, overcome a certain disgust. . . . This feeling increases to the point of causing vomiting. But if you have a schnapps, the feeling can be suppressed and you can work. If you must work in a place where there are corpses already in a state of decay, you get a very bad taste in your mouth. But this too can be curbed if you have a schnapps. Cigarette smoke works well, too—not while you are working, because then the cigarette will taste bad—but during a break. Breaks are necessary every two hours, to get some fresh air. We have had the best luck with rum.[67]

Providing Babies for the *Reich*

Even as the people on the home front endured deadly air raids as well as shortages of food, clothing, shoes, and fuel for their homes, they were still expected to support the war effort and the ultimate goal of National Socialism. Indeed, Germany's goal in attacking its neighbors and dominating Europe was to achieve *lebensraum*, or living space. To the Nazis, achieving *lebensraum* meant that Poland, Czechoslovakia, France, and the other occupied countries were to be populated with Aryans, and Aryans were to be the rulers of the European continent. To achieve *lebensraum*, German couples were expected to provide the *Reich* with new citizens.

> **WORDS IN CONTEXT**
> *lebensraum*
> Living space; the plan by Nazi leaders to repopulate other European nations with the Aryan race.

In 1933, soon after Hitler assumed power, the *Reichstäg* passed the Law of the Encouragement of Marriage. The law encouraged couples to marry, providing them with a government loan of one thousand German marks—the equivalent of nine months' income to the average German worker. Some eight hundred thousand couples took advantage of the new law. Moreover, under the law the loans were forgiven if couples provided the German nation with babies. If a couple produced a single baby, the Nazi government forgave 25 percent of that couple's loan—meaning that if a young woman gave birth to four children the entire loan was forgiven. Said propaganda minister Joseph Goebbels, "The mission of women is to be beautiful and to bring children into the world. This is not at all as . . . unmodern as it sounds. The female bird pretties herself for her mate and hatches eggs for him. In exchange, the male takes care of gathering food, and stands guard and wards off the enemy."[68]

> **WORDS IN CONTEXT**
> *Lebensborn*
> Fountain of Life; homes established by the Nazi government where unmarried women resided and attempted to become pregnant by German men, usually SS officers.

A main beneficiary of the law was the German military: The more male babies that were born, the more soldiers were available for Hitler's long-range plan to attack Germany's neighbors. However, since the ultimate goal was not only to enlarge the German army but to also spread the Aryan race further into Europe, children of both genders were welcomed into Nazi society—as long as they were of Aryan descent and, therefore, racially acceptable to the Nazi regime.

The *Lebensborn* Homes

Achieving *lebensraum* was regarded as such a high priority that the Nazis did not frown on pregnancies by unwed mothers. Starting in 1936 the Nazi government established the *Lebensborn* (Fountain of Life) system. Under this system young unmarried women were given places to live; in return they were expected to engage in sexual relations with Aryan men, usually SS members.

Lebensborn homes, which were located in many cities, were by no means regarded as brothels. They were not secret buildings hidden away on side streets but attractive, well-kept residences that were well-publicized by the government. The front of each *Lebensborn* home was adorned with a large white flag with a red dot in the middle of the banner, identifying the building as a *Lebensborn* home. The *Lebensborn* project fell far short of repopulating Germany with potential members of the military or providing future Aryan citizens for German-occupied lands. In the eight years in which the Nazis pursued the *Lebensborn* project, a mere eight thousand women are believed to have given birth to new members of the Aryan race.

By 1943 the *Lebensborn* and loan programs were falling short of their goals, and battlefield losses were clearly decimating the male German population. For a time the Nazi government considered a law requiring all German women of child-bearing age to produce four babies. In addition, as part of the proposed law, a man who had already fathered four children would be encouraged to have sexual relations outside marriage as a way of replenishing the male population. Realizing that encouraging adultery would have been a socially unpopular idea, however, Nazi leaders elected not to institute the law.

Nevertheless, even as the bombs fell on German cities, women were expected to do their duty and provide babies for the *Reich*. Since the earliest days of the Nazi regime, working women were encouraged to leave their professions and become obedient housewives and, above all, mothers. Hitler was of the belief that slim women would have trouble becoming pregnant and, therefore, dieting by women was discouraged. Instead, women were encouraged to gain weight.

Women who produced babies were rewarded by the *Reich*. Each August 12 (the birthday of Hitler's mother) the German government awarded the Motherhood Cross to women who produced the most babies. The gold cross went to women who provided the *Reich* with eight children; mothers of six children received the silver cross, while the bronze cross was awarded to mothers of four children. During the Nazi era this rhyme was familiar to virtually all women in Germany:

Take hold of kettle, broom and pan,
Then you'll surely get a man!
Shop and office leave alone,
Your true life work lies at home.[69]

German nurses walk babies conceived under the Lebensborn *(Fountain of Life) system. Under this program young unmarried women were given places to live and expected to bear the children of Aryan men.*

Ruthless Conquerors

By the spring of 1945 Allied armies were closing in on Germany from the west while Soviet troops advanced from the east. The Soviet invaders proved themselves to be ruthless conquerors. German citizens caught in the path of the Soviets were shown no mercy. Women in cities and villages were raped, some as much as a dozen times, by Soviet soldiers. One victim was Gabriele Köpp, who lived with her family in the town of Schneidemühl in the German region of Pomerania. (Today the town is known as Pila and is located in northwestern Poland.) In January 1945, as Soviet soldiers advanced toward her town, Köpp—then just fifteen years old—packed her clothes and prepared to flee. The next day Köpp and an older sister fled their house as Soviet artillery shells fell on Schneidemühl. The sisters boarded a freight train, but the train had barely left the town when it stopped. The locomotive was struck and disabled by a Soviet shell. Köpp found the doors of the freight car locked but, as a slim and athletic girl, was able to hoist herself through a narrow window near the ceiling of the car. Her sister was unable to escape—and Köpp never saw her again.

Köpp and other refugees from the train trudged through the snow, finding shelter in a nearby village. But the Soviet soldiers soon arrived and immediately rounded up all the women. Shoved into a village house, Köpp was raped by two men. The next morning, Köpp was tossed into a barn and raped again by two Soviet soldiers.

She endured this ordeal over the next two weeks, the victim of repeated sexual assaults by Soviet soldiers. At the end of that two-week period Köpp managed to slip away, finding shelter at a nearby farm where she composed a letter to her mother: "There is no one here to come to my aid. If only you were here. I'm so afraid. . . . I'm sure you could help me. If only dear God wasn't doing this to me. Oh, dear mother, if only I hadn't left without you."[70]

Bombing of Dresden

Köpp endured a terrible ordeal, but she emerged from the war with her life. Many other German civilians did not survive the war—victims of the relentless air raids by the Allied bombing crews. Some 3.8 million German civilians lost their lives in the war. As many as 135,000 German civilians were killed in February 1945 when the German city of Dresden was virtually leveled by Allied bombing. Dresden resident Elfriede Richter describes the scene as she and her family emerged from a bomb shelter:

> The bombs had torn open the street, blasting deep craters into the pavement that hindered the fleeing people. The street surface was hot and steaming; the soles of our shoes stuck to it with every step. Brick walls collapsed with a roaring thunder, complete outer walls of houses came tumbling down onto the sidewalks in front of and behind us, while some of the bricks rolled all the way

to the center of the street. Small and large objects shot through the air came crashing down unexpectedly, throwing people to the ground. Bodies were lying in the street, some burned beyond recognition. Injured people called for help. I repeated to myself, keep going, we must get away from here, don't think about anything, don't stop, don't look! People shrieked in terror and sank down before our eyes, but how could we have helped? . . . Once we were even forced to climb over a dead person if we didn't want to get trampled down or separated ourselves.[71]

Now homeless, Richter and her family made their way out of the city. On the outskirts of Dresden they encountered a makeshift hospital where they were provided with food. "The porridge was our first hot meal since the previous day," she says. "We hadn't really noticed our hunger until we smelled the food. The helpers even filled the baby bottle with warm milk. . . . As we sat on the bench with our backs toward the city, spooning up our hot oatmeal while constantly spitting out husks, I felt the warmth of food in my stomach."[72]

Teenage Boys Answer the Call

With their cities under siege and military ranks decimated, the Nazis turned to one final strategy to hold off the advancing Allied and Russian troops: Teenage boys were recruited to serve as German soldiers. On April 19, 1945, Liselotee Günzel, then just seventeen, watched many boys—some her age, but many younger—dressed in uniforms of the German army, riding their bicycles through the streets of Berlin. Their rifles were slung over their shoulders. She had mixed feelings. She was proud of the boys for answering the call to defend their homeland but knew they would be no match for the seasoned soldiers and superior weaponry of the Allied and Soviet troops. She recalls thinking, "I am so proud of our boys, who are now throwing themselves against the tanks when the order comes. But they are being hounded to their deaths."[73]

As Günzel suspected, the teenage soldiers were overwhelmed by the enemy soldiers. One of the teenage boys who answered the call to arms

Looking Back

The Bombing of Schweinfurt

According to historian Earl R. Beck, many Germans first realized the war was unwinnable in April 1943 when American bombers wiped out an important munitions factory in the city of Schweinfurt near Munich. The loss of the factory provided both a military and psychological setback for the Germans. Says Beck,

> The appearance of the American bombers flying in broad daylight across a large section of Germany had a tremendous psychological impact. This was heightened by the effects of the bombing, which revealed that even the larger edifices of the factories could be so deeply penetrated by the bombs that the cellars of the factories were no longer secure. . . .
>
> The bombs caused continuing protest and concern across Germany. "They are the talk of the day and weigh like a nightmare on the whole population," read one of the [government's] reports. Many Germans felt that the war had to be ended or all of Germany's cities would be destroyed. For many women the idea of having children under these circumstances was criminal—their fathers would fall in battle and their mothers under the rubble of the cities, and even if the children themselves did not meet an agonizing death in the bombing, they might well be left orphans, subject to the uncertain hazards of fate. Many women probably followed the reported example of one mother who remade her maternity gown into a street dress because she felt that she would have no need for the former while the war was on.

Earl R. Beck, *Under the Bombs: The German Home Front, 1942–1945.* Lexington: University of Kentucky Press, 1986, pp. 86–87.

was Alfons Heck, the avid Hitler Youth member from the town of Wittlich. In 1944, at the age of fifteen, Heck was given military training. By the next spring he had been placed in charge of a regiment of some four hundred young people, all former Hitler Youth members who were now expected to face combat.

Heck and the boys under his command were transported to the German town of Bitburg, not far from Wittlich, where they were told they would help repel an Allied siege. On their first day in Bitburg the boys dug trenches to prepare for the attack. On their second day a column of American tanks entered the town. Within minutes the Americans laid down a heavy barrage not far from where the teenagers were entrenched. "From the south . . . came the staccato of enemy gunfire," says Heck. "To my left, three Hitler Youth boys were frantically pushing a heavy machine gun over the rim of the trench."[74]

Heck was prepared to fight on, but soon his regiment of young warriors was ordered to retreat. The next day he arrived home in Wittlich. And on the following day Heck's town was captured by American troops. For Heck the war was over.

Willing Conspirators

And for all Germans the war soon ended as well. In late April 1945, with Allied and Soviet troops closing in on Berlin, Hitler committed suicide. Nazi troops held out for another week, but on May 8 the Allies declared victory, ending the war in Europe. The German people had followed Hitler and the Nazis for twelve years, accepting their vision for Germany as the dominant nation on the European continent. Their indoctrinations into Nazism commenced at early ages as they joined the Hitler Youth. They accepted the racism and barbarism and became willing conspirators in the attempted extermination of the Jews. They believed the propaganda of Goebbels, and they shrugged their shoulders as innocent people were arrested by the Gestapo. The German people paid a heavy price for entrusting the Nazis with virtually unbridled power.

Source Notes

Introduction: The Night the Nazis Burned the Books

1. Quoted in William Shirer, *The Rise and Fall of the Third Reich*. New York: Simon & Schuster, 1960, p. 241.
2. Quoted in Rebecca Mullins, *That World of Somewhere In Between: The History of Cabaret and the Cabaret Songs of Richard Pearson Thomas*, vol. 1. Ohio State University, 2013, p. 35. https://etd.ohiolink.edu.

Chapter One: The Power of Propaganda

3. Quoted in Roger Manvell and Heinrich Fraenkel, *Doctor Goebbels: His Life and Death*. e-book. New York: Skyhorse, 2010.
4. Shirer, *The Rise and Fall of the Third Reich*, p. 248.
5. Quoted in Eric A. Johnson and Karl-Heinz Reuband, *What We Knew: Terror, Mass Murder, and Everyday Life in Nazi Germany*. Cambridge, MA: Basic Books, 2005, p. 148.
6. Quoted in Shoah Resource Center, "Testimony of Stefanie S. Sucher About the Poisonous Effects of Anti-Jewish Propaganda," 2014. www.yadvashem.org.
7. Quoted in Daniel Jonah Goldhagen, *Hitler's Willing Executioners: Ordinary Germans and the Holocaust*. New York: Alfred A. Knopf, 1996, p. 179.
8. Quoted in Irene Heskes, *Passport to Jewish Music: Its History, Traditions, and Culture*. Westport, CN: Greenwood, 1994, p. 158.
9. Quoted in Randall Bytwerk, "Nazi Posters: 1933–1939," German Propaganda Archive, 2001. www.bytwerk.com.
10. Quoted in Bytwerk, "Nazi Posters: 1933–1939."
11. Quoted in Bytwerk, "Nazi Posters: 1933–1939."
12. Quoted in Johnson and Reuband, *What We Knew*, p. 163.
13. Quoted in Tilman Allert, *The Hitler Salute: On the Meaning of a Gesture*. New York: Picador, 2005, p. 10.

14. Quoted in Leni Riefenstahl, *Leni Riefenstahl: A Memoir*. New York: Picador, 1992, p. 158.

15. Quoted in Stephen Brockmann, *A Critical History of German Film*. Rochester, NY: Camden House, 2010, p. 155.

Chapter Two: The Police State

16. Philip Whitman, "The Black Terror Called Gestapo," *New York Times*, December 8, 1942, p. SM5.

17. Quoted in Robert Gerwarth, *Hitler's Hangman: The Life of Heydrich*. New Haven, CT: Yale University Press, 2011, p. 5.

18. Quoted in Johnson and Reuband, *What We Knew*, p. 10.

19. Erich Hopp, "Your Mother Has Twice Given Her Life," in Eric H. Boehm, ed., *We Survived: Fourteen Histories of the Hidden and Hunted in Nazi Germany*. Cambridge, MA: Westview, 2003, p. 98.

20. Hopp, "Your Mother Has Twice Given Her Life," p. 100.

21. Whitman, "The Black Terror Called Gestapo."

22. Quoted in Roger Moorhouse, *Berlin at War*. New York: Basic Books, 2010, p. 231.

23. Quoted in Moorhouse, *Berlin at War*, p. 231.

24. Quoted in Harvard University Internet Archive, "Full Text of 'The Sonnenburg Torture Camp,'" April 25, 1945. https://archive.org.

25. Quoted in Harvard University Internet Archive, "Full Text of 'The Sonnenburg Torture Camp.'"

26. Quoted in Harvard University Internet Archive, "Full Text of 'The Sonnenburg Torture Camp.'"

27. Quoted in History Place, "The Triumph of Hitler: The Gestapo Is Born," 2001. www.historyplace.com.

28. Quoted in History Place, "The Triumph of Hitler."

Chapter Three: Jewish Life in German Cities

29. Quoted in Shirer, *The Rise and Fall of the Third Reich*, p. 26.

30. Quoted in Johnson and Reuband, *What We Knew*, p. 181.

31. Quoted in Jürgen Matthäus and Mark Roseman, *Jewish Responses to Persecution: 1933–1938*. Lanham, MD: AltaMira Press, 2010, p. 27.

32. Quoted in Matthäus and Roseman, *Jewish Responses to Persecution*, p. 28.

33. Quoted in Matthäus and Roseman, *Jewish Responses to Persecution*, p. 29.

34. Quoted in Marion A. Kaplan, *Between Dignity and Despair: Jewish Life in Nazi Germany.* New York: Oxford University Press, 1998, p. 97.

35. Quoted in Kaplan, *Between Dignity and Despair*, p. 25.

36. US Holocaust Memorial Museum, "Oral History Bella Jakubowicz Tovey," 1990. www.ushmm.org.

37. Quoted in Saul Friedländer, *The Years of Extermination: Nazi Germany and the Jews, 1939–1945.* New York: Harper Perennial, 2007, p. 253.

38. Hopp, "Your Mother Has Twice Given Her Life," p. 103.

39. Quoted in Kaplan, *Between Dignity and Despair*, p. 204.

40. Quoted in Kaplan, *Between Dignity and Despair*, p. 207.

41. Quoted in Kaplan, *Between Dignity and Despair*, p. 207.

42. Erich Hopp, *We Survived: Fourteen Histories of the Hidden and Hunted in Nazi Germany.* Cambridge, MA: Westview, 2003, p. 113.

43. Quoted in Johnson and Reuband, *What We Knew*, pp. 44–45.

44. Quoted in Johnson and Reuband, *What We Knew*, pp. 27–28.

Chapter Four: To Be Young in Nazi Germany

45. Alfons Heck, *A Child of Hitler: Germany in the Days When God Wore a Swastika.* Phoenix, AZ: Renaissance House, 1985, p. 9.

46. Quoted in Shirer, *The Rise and Fall of the Third Reich*, p. 253.

47. Quoted in Johnson and Reuband, *What We Knew*, p. 143.

48. Quoted in Heck, *A Child of Hitler*, p. 9.

49. Heck, *A Child of Hitler*, p. 8.

50. Quoted in Johnson and Reuband, *What We Knew*, pp. 149–50.

51. Ursula Mahlendorf, *The Shame of Survival: Working Through a Nazi Childhood.* University Park, PA: Penn State Press, 2009, p. 2.

52. Quoted in Bund Deutscher Mädel, "The Belief and Beauty Society," 2011. www.bdmhistory.com.

53. Quoted in Bund Deutscher Mädel, "The Belief and Beauty Society."

54. Shirer, *The Rise and Fall of the Third Reich*, p. 256.

55. Alice Hamilton, "The Youth Who Are Hitler's Strength," *New York Times*, October 8, 1933, p. SM3.

56. Quoted in Klaus P. Fischer, *Nazi Germany: A New History.* New York: Continuum, 2003, p. 350.

Chapter Five: Life on the Home Front

57. Ilse Hertzstell Lewis, *I Was There: 1926 to 1945*. Bloomington, IL: Author House, 2011, p. 18.

58. Calvin B. Hoover, "Guns for the US—and Butter, Too," *New York Times*, February 16, 1941, p. SM3.

59. Hoover, "Guns for the US—And Butter, Too," p. SM3.

60. Quoted in Shareen Blair Brysac, *Resisting Hitler: Mildred Harnack and the Red Orchestra*. New York: Oxford University Press, 2000, pp. 303–4.

61. US Senate Committee on Military Affairs, "Elimination of German War Resources, Volumes 1–9." Washington, DC: US Government Printing Office, 1945, p. 906.

62. Hertzstell Lewis, *I Was There*, pp. 18–19.

63. Sibylle Sarah Niemoeller, *Crowns, Crosses, and Stars: My Youth in Prussia, Surviving Hitler, and a Life Beyond*. West Lafayette, IN: Purdue University Press, 2012, p. 162.

64. Hertzstell Lewis, *I Was There*, p. 44.

65. Quoted in Monica Black, *Death in Berlin: From Weimar to Divided Germany*. New York: Cambridge University Press, 2010, p. 115.

66. Quoted in Black, *Death in Berlin*, p. 116.

67. Quoted in Black, *Death in Berlin*, p. 120.

68. Quoted in Schools-History.com, "Life in Hitler's Germany," 2008. www.kenbaker.wordpress.com.

69. Quoted in Schools-History.com, "Life in Hitler's Germany."

70. Quoted in Susanne Beyer, "German Woman Writes Ground-Breaking Account of WW2 Rape," *Spiegel* Online, February 26, 2010. www.spiegel.de.

71. Quoted in Angela Thompson, *Blackout: A Woman's Struggle for Survival in Twentieth Century Germany*, e-book. Bloomington, IN: iUniverse, 2012.

72. Quoted in Thompson, *Blackout*.

73. Quoted in Nicholas Stargardt, *Witnesses of War: Children's Lives Under the Nazis*. New York: Alfred A. Knopf, 2006, pp. 302–3.

74. Heck, *A Child of Hitler*, p. 166.

For Further Research

Books

Carsten Dams, *The Gestapo: Power and Terror in the Third Reich*. Oxford, UK: Oxford University Press, 2014.

Joachim C. Fest, *Not I: Memoirs of a German Childhood*. New York: Other Press, 2014.

Sybylle Sarah Niemoeller, *Crowns, Crosses, and Stars: My Youth in Prussia, Surviving Hitler, and a Life Beyond*. West Lafayette, IN: Purdue University Press, 2012.

Curt Reiss, *Joseph Goebbels*. Stroud, UK: Fonthill, 2013.

William L. Shirer, *The Rise and Fall of the Third Reich*. New York: Simon & Schuster, 2011.

Caroline Stoessinger, *A Century of Wisdom: Lessons from the Life of Alice Herz-Sommer, the World's Oldest Living Holocaust Survivor*. New York: Spiegel & Grau, 2012.

James Wilson, *The Nazis' Nuremberg Rallies*. South Yorkshire, UK: Pen & Sword, 2014.

Websites

Bund Deutscher Mädel History (www.bdmhistory.com). A website devoted to the history of the *Bund Deutscher Mädel*—the League of German Girls. Students can find comments by former members, photographs of girls in their uniforms, and propaganda literature published to entice girls to join.

German Propaganda Archive (www.calvin.edu/academic/cas/gpa/ww2 era.htm). Maintained by Michigan-based Calvin College, the website includes several images and descriptions of the content of posters and magazine covers published by the Nazi propaganda bureau.

Triumph of the Will (www.albany.edu/writers-inst/webpages4/filmnotes /fns07n6.html). Maintained by the State University of New York, the website includes a description and critique of the Nazi propaganda film *Triumph of the Will*.

United States Holocaust Memorial Museum (www.ushmm.org). The Washington, DC–based museum includes many resources for students studying Nazi Germany. By entering the word *Gestapo* into the site's search engine, for example, students can find images of Gestapo badges and eyewitness accounts of Germans arrested by the Nazi secret police.

Yad Vashem (www.yadvashem.org). Based in Jerusalem, Israel, the organization has chronicled the Nazi persecution of the Jews. (*Yad Vashem* is a Hebrew term meaning *a place and a name*.) On the website students can find eyewitness testimony of Jews who survived the Nazi persecution.

Periodicals

Susanne Beyer, "German Woman Writes Ground-Breaking Account of WW2 Rape," *Spiegel* Online, February 26, 2010. www.spiegel.de/inter national/germany/harrowing-memoir-german-woman-writes-ground -breaking-account-of-ww2-rape-a-680354.html.

Franziska Holzschuh, "A Fuller View of Nuremberg, My Hometown," *Philadelphia Inquirer*, August 17, 2014, p. C5.

Index

Röhm, Ernst, 30
Rosenberg, Blanca, 51–52
Rust, Bernhard, 67

SA (*Sturm Abteilung,* Storm Section), 9, 30–31, **31**
Sachsenhausen, 43
salute, Nazi, 21, 22–23, **24**
Schirach, Baldur von, 37, 57
Schlabrendorff, Fabian von, 35
schools
    and book burnings at universities, 8–10
    expulsion of Jews from, 17
    Nazification of, 67–68
    treatment of Jews in, 44–46
Shirer, William L., 15, 64–65
shoes, 72, 73
"Sieg Heil!" ("Hail Victory!"), 22
slogans, 20
Social Democratic Party, 29–30
Socialists, 8, 10
"Song of Germany" ("Deutschlandlied"), 18
Sonneburg prison, 37, 39–40
Soviet military, 80–81
SS (*Schutzstaffel,* Protection Squadron), 31
    See also Gestapo
Star of David, 49, **50**
Stormtroopers (SA), 9, 30–31, **31**
Streicher, Julius, 15
Sturm Abteilung (SA), 9, 30–31, **31**
Sucher, Stefanie, 17
swastika, 23
symbol(s)
    dagger as, 56
    eagle as, 34
    Hitler and design of, 26
    Nazi (Hitler) salute as, 21, 22–23, **24**
    Star of David as, 49, **50**
    swastika as, 23

torture techniques of Gestapo, 34–37, 39–40
total blackout requirement, 73
Treaty of Versailles, 25
Triumph of Will (film), 25, 27
truncheon, defined, 42

underground Jews, 51–52
undesirables
    burning of books written by, 8
    Germany to be cleansed of, 10
    sent to concentration camps, 44
universities, book burned at, 8–10
Urgent Call for Unity (1932), 9
US Constitution, 14

Versailles, Treaty of, 25

Wachsmann, Nikolaus, 38
Wessel, Horst, 18
Whitman, Philip, 20, 34
women, Nazi portrayal of Aryan, 18, **19**
World War I
    conditions in Germany after, 12
    famine during, 69
    Jews during, 42
    propaganda about, 15
World War II
    beginning of, 69
    German military during
        food for, **71**
        teenage soldiers in, 82, 84
    and goal of *lebensraum,* 77
    homefront during
        Allied bombings of, 72, 73–75, **76**, 77,
            81–82, 83
        clothing and consumer goods rationing for,
            69, 71–73
        food rationing for, 69–71
        Soviet advance on, 80–81
    occupied territories during, **11**

youth
    adoration of Hitler by, 61, 63
    book burnings and, 8–10
    effects of propaganda on, 22
    importance of, 68
    Labor Service organization for, 64–65, **65**
    portrayal of Aryan, **19**
    sexual assaults on, 81
    as soldiers, 82, 84
    treatment of Jewish, 44–46
    See also Hitler Youth

Picture Credits

Cover: Naziism. Burning of books unrelated with regime/Photo © Tarker/Bridgeman Images

Maury Aaseng: 11

Associated Press: 80

© Bettmann/CORBIS : 36, 43, 48

Thinkstock Images: 6, 7

Weekly paper *Der Sturmer*, May 1934. Front page/Photo © Tarker/ Bridgeman Images: 16

Advertisement for a German public information brochure titled "Healthy Parents—Healthy Children!," 1934 (color litho)/Deutsches Historisches Museum, Berlin, Germany/© DHM/Bridgeman Images: 19

Lustgarten Rally of the Hitler Youth on 1st May 1933, from 'Germany Awakened; (color litho, German School, (20th Century)/Private Collection/The Stapleton Collection/Bridgeman Images: 24

SA Brown shirts on parade, Reichsparteitag, Nuremberg, 1933 (photo), German Photographer (20th Century)/Private Collection/Peter Newark Military Pictures/ Bridgeman Images: 31

SA soldiers blocking the entrance to a Jewish-owned shop, Berlin, 1933 (b/w photo), German Photographer (20th Century)/© SZ Photo/Bridgeman Images: 33

Star of David Badge, 1941 (textile), German School, (20th Century)/© Galerie Bilderwelt/Bridgeman Images: 50

Hitler Youth parade circa 1936/Universal History Archive/UIG/Bridgeman Images : 58

Hitler Youth (female members) at rally c. 1934/Universal History Archive/UIG/ Bridgeman Images: 62

Members of the Reichsarbeitsdienst (Reich Labour Service) at work (b/w photo), German Photographer, (20th century)/Private Collection/© Look and Learn/Elgar Collection/Bridgeman Images: 65

A German field kitchen on the Eastern Front, 1941–44 (b/w photo), German Photographer, (20th century)/Private Collection/The Stapleton Collection/Bridgeman Images: 71

Soldiers and volunteers clear rubble after an air raid in Germany, 1942–45 (b/w photo), German Photographer, (20th century)/Private Collection/Bridgeman Images: 75

About the Author

Hal Marcovitz is a former newspaper reporter and columnist. A resident of Chalfont, Pennsylvania, he is the author of more than 170 books for young readers. His other title in the Living History series is *Life in the Time of Shakespeare*.